Roland Houde | Jerome J. Fischer
Handbook of Logic

Roland Houde | Jerome J. Fischer

Handbook of Logic

editiones scholasticae

Bibliographic information published by Deutsche Nationalbibliothek
The Deutsche Nationalbibliothek lists this publication in the Deutsche Nationalbibliographie;
detailed bibliographic data is available in the Internet at http://dnb.ddb.de

Reprint of the first edition 1954

©2013 editiones scholasticae
P.O. Box 15 41, D-63133 Heusenstamm
www.editiones-scholasticae.de

ISBN 978-3-86838-530-4

2013

No part of this book may be reproduced, stored in retrieval systems or transmitted
in any form or by any means, electronic, mechanical, photocopying, microfilming, recording or otherwise
without written permission from the Publisher, with the exception of any material supplied specifically for the
purpose of being entered and executed on a computer system, for exclusive use of the purchaser of the work.

Printed on acid-free paper
This hardcover binding meets the International Library standard

Printed in Germany
by CPI Buchbücher.de GmbH

ACKNOWLEDGEMENTS

The writers owe a general debt of gratitude to their friends and colleagues for their spirit of encouragement which has been no small help in the planning and execution of this book. A special debt of gratitude is owed by them to the Rev. Robert P. Russell, O.S.A., Ph.D., for his reading of the manuscript and for the scholarly and constructive advice given by him on so many occasions; to the Rev. Edward M. Dwyer, O.S.A., Ph.D., and Drs. James F. O'Brien and Edward J. Monahan of Villanova University and Charles F. Ferraro of Fordham University for their generous criticisms and suggestions; to Margaret M. Henrich and Mary A. Dorrian of the Villanova University Library staff for their help in the many library problems connected with the book; and, lastly, to Florette Houde for her work in preparing the typescript and for an encouragement and inspiration not easily described in words.

R. H.
J. J. F.

Villanova, Pennsylvania
November, 1953

CONTENTS

TO THE INSTRUCTOR xiii

INTRODUCTION

Where Logic Fits 1
The Why of Logic 1
What Kind of Logic 2
What "Philosophical" Logic Is 2
Whence Logic 3
And Now a Definition 4
To the Student, a Revelation 5
Footnotes 8
Supplementary Readings 8
List of References for Orientation 9

PART ONE: LOGIC OF DEFINITION

The First Act of the Mind as a Mind

SIMPLE APPREHENSION

Chapter I: The Nature of the Act

The Why of the Act 15
The Definition of the Act 15
The Proper Object of the Act 18
The Psychology of the Act 18
To the Student, an Observation 19
Supplementary Readings 21

Chapter II: The Internal Product of the Act: The Concept

The Concept Defined 22
Logical Properties of the Concept 22
    Comprehension 22
    Extension 24
Division of Concepts 24
Supplementary Readings 26

Chapter III: The Sign of the Concept: The Term

The Sign 28
    Necessity of Signs 28
    Sign Defined 29
    Division of Signs 29
The Term Defined 30
Division of Terms 30
Properties of Terms 32
To the Student, an Exhortation 34
Supplementary Readings 34

Chapter IV: Modes of Knowing Proper to the First Act

Why "Modes of Knowing" 37
Definition 37
    Definition Defined 37
    Kinds of Definitions 38
    A Good Definition 39
Division 39
    Definition of Division 39
    Kinds of Division 40
    A Good Division 40
Supplementary Readings 41
Footnotes to Part One 42

PART TWO: LOGIC OF PROPOSITIONS
The Second Act of the Mind
JUDGMENT

Chapter V: The Nature of the Act

Why the "Second" Act 45
The Psychology of Judgment 46
The Judgment Defined 46
Components of Judgments 47
Properties of Judgments 49
To the Student, a Clarification 50
Supplementary Readings 51

Chapter VI: The Internal Product of the Act: The Mental Statement

The Mental Statement Defined 53
Components of Mental Statements 53
The Rôle of the Mental Statement 54

CONTENTS ix

Chapter VII: The Sign of the Mental Statement: The Proposition

    The Proposition Defined 55
    Components of Propositions 55
    Division of Propositions 56
    Classification of Propositions into "A," "E," "I," and "O" 58
    Logical Relations of Propositions 60
        Opposition 60
        Conversion 62
        Obversion 66
    Supplementary Readings 66

Chapter VIII: Mode of Knowing Proper to the Second Act

    Immediate Inference 69
    Kinds of Immediate Inference 70
    Utility of Immediate Inference 70
    To the Student, an Application 71
    Supplementary Readings 72
Footnotes to Part Two 72

PART THREE: LOGIC OF ARGUMENTATION

The Third Act of the Mind

REASONING

Chapter IX: The Nature of the Act

    The Psychology of Reasoning 77
    Reasoning Defined 78
    Kinds of Reasoning 79
    To the Student, an Elaboration 79

Chapter X: The Internal Product of the Act: Mental Argumentation

    Mental Argumentation Defined 81
    Components of Mental Argumentation 81
    Division of Mental Argumentation 82
    The Universal Law of Argumentation 83

Chapter XI: The Sign of Argumentation: The Syllogism

    The Syllogism Defined 84
    The Deductive Syllogism 84

CONTENTS

Defined 84
Universal Principles 85
Categorical or Assertoric Syllogism 86
Figures and Moods of Categorical Syllogisms 87
Integration of Moods and Figures 89
Perfect Figure, Perfect Moods, and Perfect Syllogism 90
Modal Syllogisms 92
The Enthymeme 92
Sorites 93
Compound Syllogisms 93
Kinds of Compound Syllogisms 94
Polysyllogism 95
Classification of Deductive Syllogisms 95
Fallacies in Deductive Reasoning 96
The Inductive Syllogism 97
Defined 97
Universal Principle 98
Insufficient and Sufficient Induction 98
Supplementary Readings 99
Footnotes to Part Three 101

PART FOUR: CONTEMPORARY PROBLEMS

Scientific Method

The Old and the New

Logical Positivism

Propaganda

Chapter XII: The Scientific Method

The Rôle of Induction in Human Reason 105
Some Preliminaries to a Definition of Scientific Method 105
The Scientific Method Defined 106
The Three-Fold Manner of Inductive Inference 108
Observation 108
Experimentation 109
    Defined 109
    Experimental Techniques 109
Analogy 112
Scientific Concepts 114
The Scientific Method at Work 115
Supplementary Readings 116

CONTENTS

Chapter XIII: The Old and the New

To the Student, an Explanation 121
Traditional Logic 122
The New Logic 122
Semantics 125
Paradox 128
Supplementary Readings 129

Chapter XIV: Logical Positivism

Again, Preliminaries to a Definition 136
And Now, the Definition 138
The Limitations of Logical Positivism 138
Logical Positivism and Traditional Logic 139
Supplementary Readings 140

Chapter XV: Propaganda

Propaganda and Logic 145
Logic and Propaganda 145
"Propaganditis", Its Care and Cure 147
Supplementary Readings 148
Footnotes to Part Four 149
Index 151

TO THE INSTRUCTOR

That all is not well, and has not been well for more than two decades, in the teaching of the science of logic on the undergraduate level is all too apparent to anyone who has followed the published opinions and counter-opinions of those who have thought long and deeply on the problem. As far back as 1931, this trenchant observation was made: "It is about time that teachers of logic in Catholic schools got together for an examination of conscience, if the majority of recent texts may be taken as an indication of the state of soul."[1]

The relegation of traditional logic to the category of a dead science or a quaint historical curiosity in many, if not most, of the curricula of our contemporary institutions of higher learning, the impact of modern or symbolic logic on the traditional — these have left too many educators in the scholastic tradition confused, introverted, even afraid. What is to be made of it all? What is to be done?

Those outside the traditions of Scholasticism, the teachers of philosophy in our secular institutions, have, in many cases, not dodged the issues. In one of the papers written as part of a study "of the present state of philosophy and of the rôle philosophy might play in the postwar world" undertaken by the American Philosophical Association in 1943 and published in 1945 under the title *Philosophy in American Education*,[2] this observation was made: "The traditional undergraduate course in logic . . . takes slight account of modern developments. It goes on discussing in the usual way terms, definition and division, propositions, syllogisms, fallacies, and the methods of induction — the latter, mostly as conceived by Mill."

Reason enough is this, for some, for replacing the traditional course by one in symbolic (i.e. mathematical) logic. When this is done, the report of the Association goes on to say, "one hears that the students go through the course as well, perhaps, as through one in mathematics, but with only a hazy idea of what it is all about or may be good for." This is so despite the fact that symbolic logic, the report goes on to note, "exploring as it does the hidden anatomy of human reason, and revealing the amazing extent of its latent powers — can be and, by its best teachers, is presented in quite as illuminating and dramatic a manner as can be others of the more rigorous college subjects." Nevertheless, the question remains, suggests Professor Ducasse, the writer of the paper, "as to whether even the best-taught course in symbolic logic provides the sort of experience of logic most profitable to an undergraduate not likely to make any further study of the subject. . . . Viewing this question from the standpoint of the objectives of liberal education, it would seem that what the student chiefly needs to gain from logic in college is enhanced capacity to carry on soundly and to criticize effectively the reasonings connected with matters he will have to think about: that is, reasonings connected with his private concerns, with public affairs, and with his other studies. But these reasonings are in the great majority of cases carried on in the words of ordinary language, not in the symbols of the algebra of logic; in contexts often highly emotional rather than calm. . . ." It "seems clear" then to Ducasse that, "for the purpose of discipline in such reasonings, a course in symbolic logic is not likely to be of much more service than a course in calculus would be for the purpose of figuring one's income tax." This is why, perhaps, he notes finally, "The answer would appear to be that the task calls for a course somewhat different from both extremes, but nearer to the traditional type in several respects."

TO THE INSTRUCTOR

This is the attitude of the teacher of logic outside the Catholic schools. What is the attitude of the Catholic educator?

"How Is Scholastic Logic Facing Modern Logic?" is the title of a doctoral dissertation completed at the University of Pittsburgh in the spring of 1952.[3] The writer of it, Frank C. Dillhoff, undertook a comprehensive survey of what is going on in the field of logic and the teaching of logic in "every known Catholic institution of higher learning in the world." To be sure, not all the schools coöperated in the investigation undertaken, but enough of them did to enable the researcher to arrive at several revealing conclusions. Among the most significant, and for present purposes the most pertinent, is "the conclusion that there is considerable evidence for a forthcoming change in the attitude within the field of Scholastic logic," suggested by the recognition of "the undeveloped state of the logic of Aristotle and St. Thomas, which therefore needs completion." Concerning this conclusion, says Dr. Dillhoff, "there were repeated allusions to the need of a 'complete text' for teaching Scholastic logic."

It would seem from the foregoing that both in and outside the Scholastic tradition the view of educators is that there is a need for a new approach in teaching logic to the undergraduate student — a need, it would seem, for a new kind of text and for a new or at least modified method of presentation. The traditional text in Scholastic logic, which "takes slight account of modern developments," and which in some cases blithely ignores induction altogether, would appear to be deficient. The substitution of mathematical logic for the traditional, the outright replacing of the latter by the former, might be compared to forsaking brick and mortar as outmoded in view of plastics.

Out of this background of thinking the idea for the present book has grown. Extravagant, indeed, would be the expectations of the writers, if they were to presume here that they have solved the problem completely. They have attempted, in what seems to them the most practicable way, to answer the present need. This book, therefore, and the WORKBOOK OF LOGIC (by the same authors and published by the Wm. C. Brown Company, Dubuque, Iowa) which is designed to accompany it, represent the attempt to provide the student (presumably sophomore) in the one semester introductory course in logic with: 1) A *handbook* of the fundamentals of the science, brief and succinct enough to be practical and yet substantial enough to provide him with the solid foundation of the traditional from which to approach the "mysteries" of modern developments in the field. 2) A *working* knowledge of the science, out of which (with the aid of the instructor) there may be built the personal equipment with which the student may be able to solve for himself the problems posed by the impact of the new on the old in the field of logic. 3) *Sufficient* problem materials to enable the student to learn the *use of logic,* so that in reconciling in his own mind the new and the old, the modern and the traditional, he may do this *logically.*

In accordance with these general aims, the manner and the matter of the present book have not been approached with condescension or vaingloriousness. With regard to the manner: this book is not intended to be a vehicle for the display of the erudition (real or imagined) of the authors. Its language is intended to be concise, straightforward, clear. It attempts to speak not *at* the student, or *down on* him, but *to* him. It attempts further to bring together, as far as it is possible for this to be done on the introductory or sophomore level, the syntax of the language and the terminology of logic. It attempts, finally, to present logic *logically,* that is, to apply what is being taught to the student to the presentation of the subject — to explain, in short, the natural logical progression of our mental experiences or operations and to present in a compact handbook the ontological, psychological, and logical axioms (and immediate deductions from these) of clear, orderly thinking.

With regard to the matter, therefore: the HANDBOOK is accordingly divided into four major parts, the first three of which are devoted respectively to the three operations of the mind in their natural logical order, and the fourth to a presentation of contemporary developments, problems, views, etc.

> Truth fails not; but her outward forms that bear
> The longest date do melt like frosty rime,
> That in the morning whitened hill and plain
> And is no more. . . .

said the poet Wordsworth. Truth does not change, but the human expression of it does. No honest intellect can ignore the contemporary human expression of the old truths; neither can it put aside the thoughts and opinions that the great minds of the past have bequeathed us. Of the ancients, it has been said, "they help us not only by the truths which they discovered and handed down, but even by their very errors, which are useful to us insofar as they indicate the ways we are to avoid in our search for truth."[4] It is on this basis that the book attempts as far as possible to maintain a consistent parallelism between traditional principles and modern exceptions to and variations from the traditional. It is on this basis that the book, after establishing the student on the foundation of the traditional, undertakes to introduce him to contemporary concerns, in the field of mathematical logic, semantics, logical positivism, propaganda, etc.

Attention is called to the Supplementary Readings following each of the chapters of the book. It will be a serious mistake on the part of the instructor to regard these as mere academic trappings, to be used or not as the mood comes.

The readings are designed to cover the whole field of logic, to show where research, investigation, thinking has been done, is being done, or (as may be the case) has not yet been done on the various divisions of the subject presented in the HANDBOOK. They are intended to be used for a) reading reports, b) classroom discussion or interplay of ideas, c) the application of logic or critical thinking, d) acquainting the student with the people who study, formulate, and expound the science.

Lastly, the authors suggest this specific plan for the use of the HANDBOOK and accompanying WORKBOOK — one of many possible plans, to be sure, but to their way of thinking the most practicable. In the regular three-credit-hour course in the subject, the first hour of the week could be devoted to the HANDBOOK and the explication of principles, the second hour to the problem materials, the third to the Supplementary Readings (reports, discussion, etc.).

FOOTNOTES

1. C. A. Hart, *The New Scholasticism*, vol. 5, 1931, p. 181.
2. *Philosophy in American Education*, Harper & Brothers, New York, pp. 224-227.
3. F. C. Dillhoff, *How Is Scholastic Logic Facing Modern Logic?* Ph.D. Dissertation, University of Pittsburgh, 1952.
4. Thomas Aquinas, *In II Meta.*, lect. 1, n. 287-88, ed. Cathala.

INTRODUCTION

Where Logic Fits

Understanding where logic fits involves understanding where a college education fits in the life of the individual student. The traditional conception of going to college "to broaden oneself" has become in many respects a meaningless generalization. In truth, one goes to college, one reads and listens and studies, studies not merely chemistry or physics or engineering or mathematics or accounting or marketing but also that broad and not always rightly understood group of subjects called the humanities (philosophy, language, literature, history, political science, etc.) to help him to realize himself. He goes to college, it might be said, to find out what he is. Generally, he goes to college, specifically, he studies the humanities, in order to realize his human-ness.

Logic is one of the humanities. Logic is the science of thought. Concerned as it is with methods — the operations of man's prime faculty, his reason — it might indeed be said to be *the science of science.* "A student should address himself to logic before the other sciences, because it deals with their common procedure."[1] This is the advice of Thomas Aquinas. More than a thousand years before Aquinas, Aristotle said ". . . it is absurd to seek at the same time knowledge and the way of attaining knowledge. . . ."[2] Knowledge begins, in short, with logic. *Learning logic means learning how to think.*

The Why of Logic

Man finds himself constrained to think, because he is a thinking creature. Not to think, not to exercise reason, is not to realize his own nature. "Reason more than anything else," says Aristotle again, "is man."[3] It follows, then, that logic, the science or study of reason, is a thing not extrinsic to man but intrinsic to him. Logic as human experience is a part of man's *human-ness*. To be logical is to be human.

What Kind of Logic

In modern times, as a consequence of continuing alterations in the points of view among philosophers, there arises frequently a misleading notion of division between *kinds of logic*. If reason is the man, if man (that is to say) is the reasoner, and if logic is the science of reason, it might be said that logic is, as well, the science of the reasoner. When one understands the interrelationship between an object being reasoned about and the mind doing the reasoning, between the reasoned and the reasoner, between the laws of being and the laws of thought, it becomes apparent that a division between what is called "material logic" and what is called "formal logic" is, as noted, misleading. The science of logic does not divide content from form. Logic is not properly spoken of as (in one instance) *substantive* or *material* and (in another instance) *mathematical* or *formal*. The science or study of reason, which is logic, concerned as it is with man's intellect or thought processes, may be described as "psychological"; concerned as it is with the objects of his thought processes, it may be described as "ontological". In its ontological and psychological aspects logic may properly be described as "philosophical". If, then, there is a *kind* of logic, the kind with which we are dealing here is just that: *philosophical logic*.

What "Philosophical" Logic Is

Philosophy, said Aristotle, begins in wonderment.[4] It is the science of all things studied in their ultimate causes and reasons with the aid of reason alone. That which is concerned with the study of things in their ultimate causes and reasons may be described as *philosophical*. Logic, if it is the study of reason in its ultimate causes, is thus philosophical. It is philosophical if it seeks and discovers the last possible or ultimate explanations of its own parts, which are: a) the forms of thought and b) the contents of thoughts. It is more than the study of the mathematical configurations of the imagination. It asks not merely *how;* it asks also *what* and *why*. In the sense that it is philosophical, it is truly human, universal, ultimate; it transcends the individual, the local, the proximate. The patrimony of truth for the human race is *one*. If there is not one criterion of truth for the Russian, another for the Frenchman, and another for the American, then there is not a Russian logic, a French logic, an American logic. There is not one logic for John Smith and another logic for Joe Jones.

Whence Logic

Logic and psychology are different things. The province of one is not the province of the other. In so far as logic bears upon the psychological it does so out of concern for the nature of man's reason or intellect, out of concern for the processes or operations of that faculty. Logic is psychological since it seeks to explain the natural, orderly progression of man's mental experiences.

Logic and ontology likewise are different things. Logic is not ontology, but it is ontological to the extent that its first principles derive from ontology, which is the study of being *as being*. "... the most certain principle of all is that regarding which it is impossible to be mistaken. ... For a principle which everyone must have who understands anything that is is not a hypothesis; and that which everyone must know who knows anything, he must already have when he comes to a special study."⁵ There are, in other words, first principles, called in ontology "laws of being", which the student must bring to a study of any science. The laws of being precede the laws of thought.

To the study of logic the student must bring, at the very outset, the first of these laws, called "the law of contradiction" and referred to in philosophy as *the first indemonstrable*,⁶ (viz., the same attribute cannot at the same time be affirmed and denied of the same subject or being; that is to say, it is impossible simultaneously to affirm and to deny). A positive formulation of this law is "the principle of identity" — a being must always be itself. From the negative and positive formulations of the first indemonstrable derives another principle, called "the law of the excluded middle"; viz., between being and non-being there is no middle course. From this first law of being and its two adjuncts, the principle of identity and the law of the excluded middle, the science of logic proceeds.

And Now a Definition

Logic has been referred to here, so far, as human experience, the science of science, the study of reason in its ultimate causes. A proper definition of logic requires perhaps more preciseness than is to be found in such general descriptive phrases.

Among philosophers and students of philosophy logic has been variously defined as: "the method of science",⁷ "the science which investigates the general principles of valid thought",⁸ "the art which directs the very action of the mind so that man, in exercising his mind, proceeds orderly, easily, and without error."⁹ Logic, it has been said, "is made up of rules that thinking has to impose upon itself in order to be effective."[10] The function of logic, it has been further said, "is to help us to think clearly and objectively, express ourselves plainly and accurately, reason correctly and estimate aright the statements and arguments of others."[11]

To refer to logic one moment as a science and another moment as an art may be misleading. Man is a creature endowed with reason; reason or thought is, with him, a natural disposition. As such it may be spoken of as an art, a faculty to be used, developed, trained, to the end that it might realize, in man, the fullness of its own nature. Because man is capable not only of thinking but also of thinking about thinking, thought or reason may be spoken of also as a science, an observation, an investigation, a study. It is a study of method, as applied to the operations of man's intellect. But it is at the same time the method (or the sum of those methods) it uses to study method. Logic is concerned not only with the means but also with the end of the means. It is in the light of this that logic may be defined, more precisely than heretofore, as the science of correct and true thinking.

The proper object of the intellect is knowledge. And since no one but a fool would admit that he seeks *error*, knowledge here is understood to mean *true knowledge*. Logic, then is the mind's method for finding truth. It has for its object ultimate "notions" or "concepts" or "ideas", and the capacity of these to be developed and to be linked one with another, according to the law of contradiction and its two adjuncts (the principle of identity and the law of the excluded middle) out of which emerges the *first indemonstrable*, already mentioned.

To the Student, a Revelation

A cordial reception, says the educator, is a condition of learning. An attempt is being made, in these introductory pages, to explain to you what logic is, what its purpose is, and where it fits in the scheme of *your* education. Logic is one of the humanities, which one studies in order to become more truly a human being. It is the study or investigation of thought, the study of not only what thought is but also how it works. Learning logic means learning how to think. Man is obligated to think; he cannot do otherwise, if he is to realize his own human-ness. To be logical is not then to be different, to be outside the pale, to be a freak. To be logical is to be human.

Logic is with you every waking moment of the day. Indeed, without it, you could not move through the activities that occupy your day; you would move, instead, in the world of half-thoughts, anomalies, and incongruities that characterize our dreams in sleep.

When the alarm clock rings in the morning and through the haze of reawakened consciousness you heed its call, logic is already with you. In that brief moment your mind has performed the first and simplest act that it, from its nature, is capable of; you have made a *simple apprehension*.

It is seven o'clock, time to get up and be off for your first class at eight. But you are tired. You would prefer to stay abed. This was what you did yesterday. And because you did you were late and missed your class. If you stay abed, the same thing will happen today. In this brief cognizance, your mind has now performed the second and more involved act that it, from its own nature, is capable of; you have made a *judgment*, indeed several judgments.

Missing class yesterday has put you in a position of some precariousness. You have already run the limit of your allowed absences from class. One more absence, and you have cut yourself out of the course. There is no room this morning for indecision. It is seven o'clock, and you arise. In the moment that you do arise, your mind has completed the third and the most complex of the acts that it, from its own nature, is capable of; you have *reasoned*.

Perhaps you see now that logic is part of your human-ness, that it is you thinking about you. Consider for a moment what you are. A being doubly composed, a being sensory and a being intellectual. You have your senses, by which you know the reality of the sensate world outside your skin. You have your intellect or mind, by which you think about what you know. The sensory life of the human being and its relationship to the whole man is properly the concern (in certain areas) of biology and (in others) of psychology. The intellectual, the thinking life of the human being is the concern of logic.

As a study of the workings of the intellect or mind, the science of logic *logically* divides itself into three parts, according to *the three operations of the mind* in their natural order: 1) Simple Apprehension, 2) Judgment, 3) Reasoning. Logic is the science of thought. Thinking is reasoning. Reasoning is based on judgment. Judgment grows out of simple apprehension.

It is on this inescapable order of progression that the plan of this book is founded. As a student of logic you are going to proceed with first things first; you are going to study the three acts of the mind in their natural order of progression.

As a student of logic, as one engaged in the process of discovering and directing his own intellect or reason, as a potential logician or thinking adult (they are the same thing), you have need of two tools. One of these is the body of the science, its fundamentals, its parts, its fabric. The other is logic itself, the method, the thing. Indeed, you. Or that part of your human-ness which sets you above every other living creature in the natural order. You, thinking about *you*.

The first of these tools, as you will see, it is the purpose of this book to provide. The other is one over which the authors have no say. The say is yours. The tool is one you only can provide.

FOOTNOTES TO INTRODUCTION

1. Thomas Aquinas, *In II Meta.*, Lect. 5, n. 335, ed. Cathala.
2. *Meta.*, 995 a 12-15.
3. *Nico. Ethics*, 1178 a 7; 1169 a 1.
4. *Meta.*, 982 b 12.
5. *Meta.*, 1005 a 19ff.
6. *S.T.*, I a II ae, q. 94, a. 2.
   Plato, *Republic*, 437a.
   An. Post. 77a 10.
   Meta., 1005 b 23-31.
   Contra Gentes II, c. 83.
   George Boole, *Collected Logical Works*, vol. II, "The Laws of Thought," University of Chicago Press, Chicago, 1940, pp. 53-55.
   Jacques Maritain, *A Preface to Metaphysics*, London, 1948, p. 91.
7. Boethius, in Thomas Aquinas Opusc. XVI, Expositio, *De Trinitate*, v, 1, ad 2.
8. John N. Keynes, *Formal Logic*, Macmillan Co., Introd., p. 1.
9. *Comm., An. Post.*, lib. I, lect. 1.
10. Monroe C. Beardsley, *Practical Logic*, Prentice-Hall, New York, 1950, p. XIII.
11. Herbert A. Aikins, *The Principles of Logic*, Henry Holt and Co., New York, 1902, ch. 1.

SUPPLEMENTARY READINGS FOR INTRODUCTION

Avey, A. E., "The Law of Contradiction: Its Logical Status," *Journal of Philosophy*, vol. 26, (September, 1929), pp. 519-526.

Boehner, P., *Medieval Logic*, University of Chicago Press, Chicago, 1952, pp. xi - xviii.

Bogoslovsky, B. B., *The Technique of Controversy*, Harcourt, Brace and Co., New York, 1928, pp. 36-71.

Burtt, E. A., *Principles and Problems of Right Thinking*, rev. ed., Harper and Brothers, New York, 1931, pp.3-31.

Creedy, F., *Logic as the Cross-Classification and Selection of Arbitrary Elements*, Lehigh University, Bethlehem, Pennsylvania, 1931.

Guthrie, E. R., "The Field of Logic," *Journal of Philosophy*, vol. 13, (March, 1916), pp. 152-157.

Kimpel, B. F., *A Critique of the Logic of Contradiction as the Exclusive Principle of Interpretation in an Idealistic Metaphysic*, Mennonite Press, Scottdale, Pennsylvania, 1934.

McGill, V. J., "Concerning the Laws of Contradiction and Excluded Middle," *Philosophy of Science*, vol. 6, 1939, pp. 196-211.

Montague, W. P., *The Ways of Things*, Prentice-Hall, New York, 1940, pp. 3-18.

Nagel, E., "Logic without Ontology," *Naturalism and the Human Spirit*, ed. Y. H. Krikorian, Columbia University Press, New York, 1944, pp. 210-241.

Negley, G. R., *The Organization of Knowledge*, Prentice-Hall, New York, 1942, pp. 3-17.

Popov, P. S., "The Logic of Aristotle and Formal Logic," *Philosophy and Phenomenological Research*, vol. 8, (September, 1947), pp. 1-22.

Reiser, O., *Humanistic Logic*, Thomas Y. Crowell, New York, 1930, pp. 17-30, pp. 70-74, pp. 81-112.

Toms, E., "The Law of Excluded Middle," *Philosophy of Science*, vol. 8, 1941, pp. 33-38.

LIST OF REFERENCES FOR ORIENTATION

Dictionaries:

Diccionario de Filosofia
Jose Mora Ferrater
Buenos Aires, 1951

The Dictionary of Philosophy
Editor, Dagobert D. Runes
Philosophical Library, New York, 1942

Dictionary of Philosophy and Psychology
Editor, James Mark Baldwin
3 vols., New York: Macmillan Co., 1901

Dizionario di Scienze Filosofiche
C. Ranzoli
Ulrico Hoepli, Milano, 1916

Vocabulaire Technique et Critique de la Philosophie
André Lalande
Presses Universitaires de France, Paris, 1947

Journals:

Diogenes
An International Review of Philosophy and Humanistic Studies, published quarterly by the Int. Council for Philosophy in association with UNESCO.

Dominican Studies
Quarterly Review of Theology and Philosophy, Blackfriars Publications, St. Giles, Oxford, England.

Franciscan Studies
Quarterly Review, St. Bonaventure, New York

The Journal of Philosophy
Published by the Journal of Philosophy, Inc., Columbia University.

The Journal of Symbolic Logic
Published quarterly by the Association for Symbolic Logic, Baltimore.

Mind
Quarterly Review of Psychology and Philosophy, T. Nelson & Sons Ltd., Edinburgh.

The Modern Schoolman
Quarterly Journal of Philosophy, Saint Louis University.

The New Scholasticism
Journal of the American Catholic Philosophical Association, The Catholic University of America, Washington, D. C.

The Philosophical Review
Ed. by the Faculty of the Sage School of Philosophy, Cornell University, Cornell University Press, Ithica, New York.

Philosophy
The Journal of the Royal Institute of Philosophy, Macmillan & Co., London.

Philosophy of Science
Quarterly publication, organ of the Philosophy of Science Association, The Williams & Wilkins Co., Baltimore, Md.

Philosophy and Phenomenological Research
A quarterly Journal, Published for the International Phenomenological Society by the University of Buffalo, Buffalo, New York.

Proceedings of the American Catholic Philosophical Association
The Catholic University of America, Washington, D. C.

The Review of Metaphysics
A Philosophical Quarterly, Yale University, New Haven, Conn.

Studies
Irish Quarterly Review of Letters, Philosophy & Science, Dublin: Ireland.

The Thomist
A Speculative Quarterly Review, The Thomist Press, Washington, D. C.

Part One

LOGIC OF DEFINITION

The First Act of the Mind as a Mind

SIMPLE APPREHENSION

CHAPTER I

The Nature of the Act

The Why of the Act

It will be noted that in the heading to Part One simple apprehension is referred to as the first act of *the mind as a mind*. What, now, is this *mind*? It is that in us by which we know that we know. But let it be understood at the beginning that, as some philosophers have told us, no man can perceive his own mind. The mind is a conclusion and not a premise; it is a thing inferred rather than "seen" or known as an object of perception. As this is so of the mind, it is so also of the operations or acts of the mind. Mental products are the manifestations of our mental life. They manifest that the mind is at work, that it is acting. This is the way, and the only way, we know the act of apprehension. It is, moreover, the *first* act because it is the one out of which the others grow and upon which they depend. It is the point at which mental life begins.

The Definition of the Act

Simple apprehension may be defined as that act by which the mind grasps or lays hold of an object, without affirming or denying anything about it. Apprehension is mental consciousness. It is the operation by which the mind *takes* (from the Latin *apprehendere*) becomes aware of, recognizes, or contemplates objects.

What are objects? Objects are all things that have being. And of all the objects which the mind is capable of apprehending the first is *being* itself. The mind can think only of what is: everything that presents itself to the mind presents itself as "being". But being is two-fold. It is, on the one hand, real; it is, on the other hand, mental or conceptual. Real being is being *outside the mind*. It may be "actual" (a chair, a child, a symphony); it may be "possible" or "potential" (a chair not yet constructed, a child not yet conceived, a symphony not yet written). Mental or conceptual being is being *within the mind*. It may be "fictional" or without foundation in nature (a chimera, a centaur, a golden mountain). It may be "veritable" or with foundation in nature.

Veritable mental being may be described, as in the case of "error" and "nothingness", as *negative;* it may be described, as in the case of "blindness" and "deafness", as *privative*. All other veritable mental beings or objects may properly be described as *positive*. These themselves are of two kinds: a) mathematical (the symbol π, irrational numbers, etc.), b) logical (the concept, the term, the proposition, the syllogism, etc.).

These *logical* veritable mental beings or objects, let us stop to note, are what the mind forms when it acts. They are the forms of thought. They are the products of the intelligence, over and above its normal function of knowing things or beings. They are themselves the *logical entities* which constitute the proper objects of the science of Logic.

Thus it is seen that, while apprehension is an act of the mind (the act of knowing or being aware), apprehension is itself one of these logical veritable mental objects or beings. As such it has the following characteristics: 1) It is *simple;* as a mental act it is incomplete and does not satisfy the mind. 2) It is *indifferent;* it is not concerned with logical truth or falsity. 3) It is *static;* it neither affirms nor denies. Some prevailing synonyms for *apprehension* are: *attention, concentration, analysis, consideration, isolation, focusing*.

LOGIC OF DEFINITION

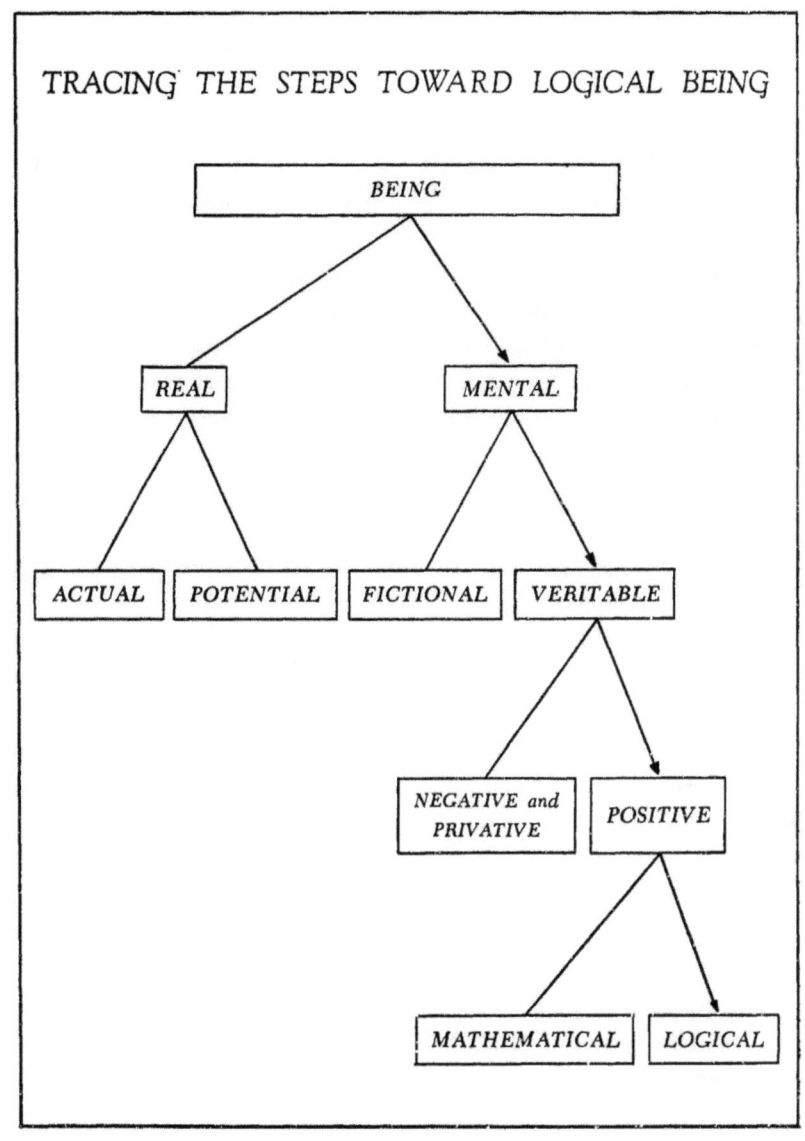

The Proper Object of the Act

A thing is said to be "proper" when it fits or belongs to something else by natural association. In this sense, the proper object of apprehension is the essence or *quiddity* of thing.[1] When the mind apprehends a tree, it grasps or lays hold of, becomes aware of or recognizes, a mental form or meaning.[2] This form or meaning is not the tree itself but an essence or quiddity abstracted from the sense image by means of which the mind makes contact with the tree outside itself. That which comes to the mind, then, in the act of apprehending is a thing proper or peculiar to it, which the mind itself begets, a something internal to itself, an object of thought.

It is with this object of thought, this essence, or meaning that thinking, or indeed knowledge, may be said to begin. We may be said to *know* a thing only when we have reduced it to its essence — indeed, only when we are aware that we have reduced it to its essence; when, in other words, we know that we know it. You may, for example, read this printed page, but to read it is not to know it. The ability to read is different from the ability to think about what is read. If you read here a word of advice for yourself, then you have read correctly.

The Psychology of the Act

In regard to the relationship between the mind (which knows) and the things outside it (which it is capable of knowing) we may speak of a two-fold order; viz., *the order of nature*, the order of things or real beings outside the mind, and the *order of knowledge*, itself divided into the "sensible" and the "intelligible". When thought occurs and the mind *knows*, it might be said that what takes place is a transference from the order of nature to the intelligible level of the order of knowledge. Let us follow, for a moment, the process of apprehension. Let us observe you apprehending.

Here before you is this book, an assemblage of printed pages between cloth covers. It is a thing or real being in the order of nature outside your mind. It enters the order of knowledge first on the sensible level. You are aware of it because your eyes see it and your hands touch it; it is with you as a sensation, that is to say an impression attained solely by the use of your external senses. The transference, if we can suppose a chronology in the process, goes further; your internal senses make of the sensation an image or *phantasm*. This now is apprehension, on the sensory level. It is as far as the process would go, if you were a lower animal. Because you are not, there is a further transference to the level of the intelligible, where in that part of you described as your active intellect there takes place a dematerializing or abstraction — a distillation, as it were — of the phantasm to produce an *impressed likeness* of the thing, this book before you on the table. Supposing chronology again, there is yet another step, as, in that part of you described as your passive intellect, out of the impressed likeness there is produced an *expressed likeness*, a notion, an idea of the book. This end product of the act of simple apprehension we call the *concept*.

To the Student, an Observation

From the foregoing chapter one thing, above all others, ought to be understood and emphasized. Perhaps, in the welter of details, you have overlooked it. The fabric of human existence, the stuff of life, the materials of sense experience, indeed, the contents of the mind, are not things about which in their particular regards it is always possible to be clear or to be certain. But this much is sure: there *are* things, and there *are* minds. This, it may be said, is our *second in-*

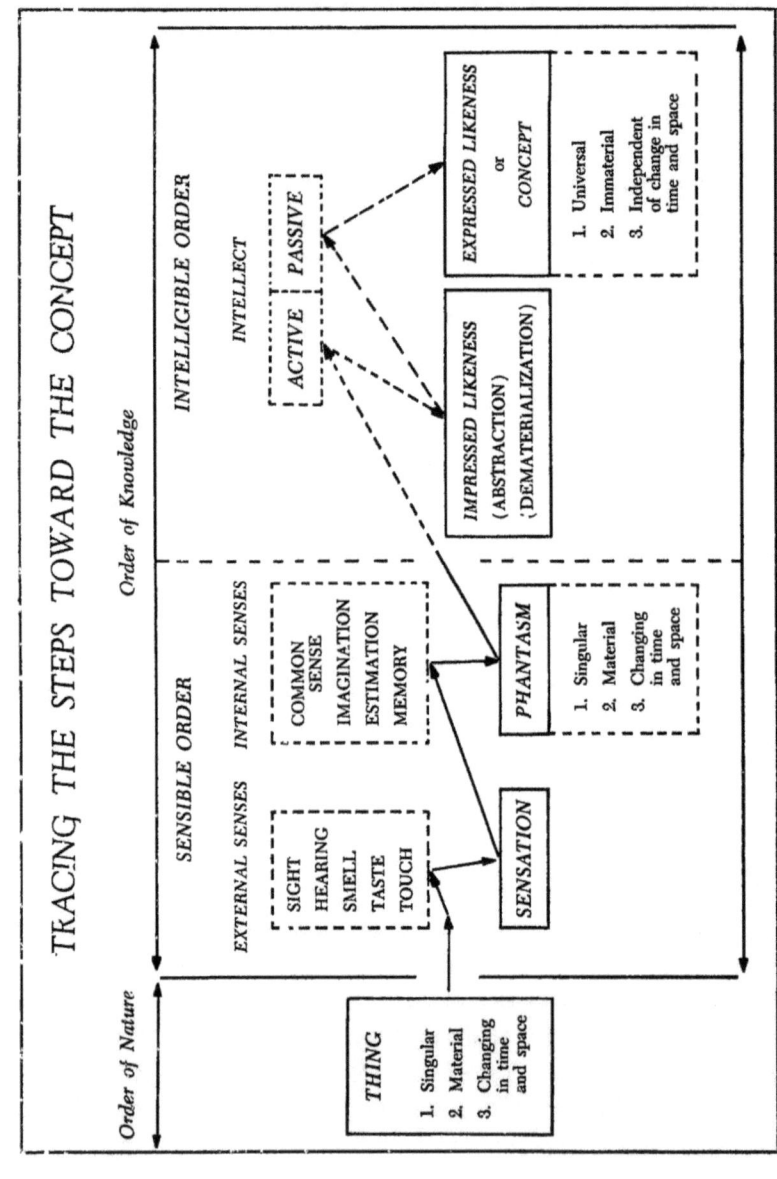

demonstrable. Whereas the first,[3] it will be remembered, was abstract, this is concrete. Let it be remembered, along the way, as well, that there is your mind and there are the minds of other human beings around you. It is the nature of the mind to seek knowledge, to try to know. Of no one, more than of the logician (that is you), might we expect a wholesome tolerance of the free working of the minds of others.

SUPPLEMENTARY READINGS FOR CHAPTER I

Bourke, V. J., "The Operations Involved in Intellectual Conception," *The Modern Schoolman,* vol. 21, 1944, pp. 83-90.

Broad, C. D., *The Mind and Its Place in Nature,* Harcourt, Brace and Co., New York, 1925.

Connolly, F. G., "Abstraction and Moderate Realism," *The New Scholasticism,* vol. 27, (January, 1953), pp. 72-90.

MacPartland, J., "Communism and the Cult of Nonbeing," *The Modern Schoolman,* vol. 26, 1949, pp. 337-340.

Moore, T. V., "The Scholastic Theory of Perception," *The New Scholasticism,* vol. 7, 1933, pp. 222-238.

O'Mara, J., "The Meaning and Value of Existentialism," *Studies,* vol. 40, 1951, pp. 11-22.

Sprague, R. K., "The Ontological Significance of Negation," *Journal of Philosophy,* vol. 44, (March, 1947), pp. 179-184.

Van Der Veldt, J., "Historical Landmarks in the Theory of Intelligence," *Franciscan Studies,* vol. 10, 1950, pp. 344-382.

Walsh, F. A., "Phantasm and Phantasy," *The New Scholasticism,* vol. 9, 1935, pp. 116-133.

Wild, J., "What Is Realism," *Journal of Philosophy,* vol. 44, (March, 1947), pp. 152-154.

Woodworth, R. S., "Imageless Thought," *Journal of Philosophy,* vol. 3, December, 1906, pp. 701-708.

CHAPTER II

The Internal Product of the Act: The Concept

The Concept Defined

The concept has been referred to, in the preceding chapter, as the end product of the act of simple apprehension. It is a product in the sense that it is something the mind produces, makes, or forms. It is an internal product because it exists *within* the mind. The concept may thus be defined as the representation of a thing expressed in the mind and by the mind, the representation by which our mind grasps or apprehends a thing, the form of a thing apart from the thing itself. Synonymous expressions for the concept are: the idea, the notion, the principle of knowledge, the "mental word".

The concept is at the same time the end of our apprehensive knowledge and the means of knowing extra-mental things or objects. It is an object of thought that may be considered in and of itself without reference to anything else.[4] That the concept and the object or thing from which it derives are not the same, should be noted. That the concept and the mind which conceives are not the same, should also be noted. The concept is that which comes to the mind when the mind knows that it knows.

Logical Properties of the Concept

The concept is said to have two logical properties. These are called: comprehension and extension.

Comprehension:

A being, now, is a whole composed of *notes* but forming a nature which is one. The notes of a being are those characteristics, aspects, attributes, or parts which, taken together, distinguish it from all other beings. They are that without which a thing would not be what it is. Man, for example, is a being composed of (among others) the notes *animal* and *rational*. But man is not two things; his notes are multiple, his nature one. The same, now, is true of the *concept of man*.

If the concept is, as pointed out, the representation in the mind of a thing grasped or apprehended, then the concept, like the thing, is composed of characteristics, aspects, attributes, parts, or notes. The sum total of the notes of a concept is called its *comprehension*.

Three things need especially to be noted about the comprehension of a concept. In the first place, the notes which give to the nature of the concept its identity and unity are *essential* ones as distinguished from *accidental* ones. That is essential which is necessary to the whole and whose removal or alteration would destroy its wholeness. That is accidental which is a part of but not necessary to the whole. In the second place, the comprehension of a concept must be understood to include not only the essential notes but also the essential "properties" of the thing of which the concept is a representation in the mind. Properties are distinct from notes in that properties emerge or flow, as it were, from the essence or quiddity of a thing but are not the essence or quiddity. (Example: Man's ability to laugh) In the third place, except for the case of himself and *his* notes, man cannot always be certain that he knows *all* the notes of a concept.[5] If the ant, for instance, could communicate to man, it is not impossible that man's concept of ant might become more comprehensive, that more notes might be added to the concept. Of those notes that man does know, in the case of a particular concept, this much, however, can be said of them: 1) They are *objective;* they derive from the thing. 2) They are *invariable;* they remain constant and unchanged. 3) They are *necessary;* they cannot be removed. 4) They are *empirical;* they are arrived at inductively; that is to say, they are the data of experience.

Extension:

Although the notes of a concept are multiple, its nature, as has been shown, is one. We may thus speak of the unity of concept. It is not, now, contradictory but complementary that we may speak also of the *universality* of a concept. Concepts when abstracted and then reflected upon are seen to be universal in the sense that they are extendable to, or are the representations of, all objects possessing the same notes. The concept man, for instance, is extendable to, or may be the representation of, all men — John Smith, Mrs. John Smith, John Smith, Jr., as well as Junior's friends Tom, Dick, and Harry. The concept chair is extendable to every chair, whether it be a Louis Quinze, a New England Colonial, or Grandpa's milking stool. This extendability or inclusiveness of the concept is called its *extension.* The extension, more formally, may be defined as the group of objects of thought or the multitude of individual things with which a concept agrees or to which it applies.

Lastly, it is to be noted that the comprehension and extension of a concept stand in inverse ratio to each other. The greater the comprehension of a concept, the less its extension; and the greater the extension, the less the comprehension.[6]

Division of Concepts

We have spoken so far, from a general standpoint, of the concept itself — what it is, what its logical properties are, and what relationship exists between these properties. What, then, of the *kinds* of concepts? How do they differ from one another?

Concepts are divided on the basis of a) their comprehension, b) their extension, c) their mutual relations, d) the degree of perfection of their representation.

(a) On the basis of their comprehension, concepts are said to be *simple* or *complex*. A simple concept is a concept that has one nature. (Caution: one "nature", not one "note")[7] Examples of the simple concept are: man, woman, chair. Simple concepts themselves are of two kinds: concrete and abstract. A concrete concept is one comprising both *form* or essence and *matter* (a man, a woman, a chair). It is a concept of a thing whose form is realized in matter. An abstract concept is one consisting, as it were, of form but not of matter (humanity, man-ness, chair-ness). It is a concept of a thing whose form is *abstracted* from individualized matter. A complex concept is one that has more than one nature; that is to say, it has a multiplicity of natures or essences grouped together. Examples of complex concepts are: honest man, clever woman, butcher, baker, wooden chair, iron stool, etc. It should be noted that, although the complex concept in the act of apprehension is grasped as one (a multiplicity in unity), its several natures may be further abstracted and reflected upon separately.

(b) On the basis of their extension, concepts may be said to be *imprecise* or *precise*. An imprecise concept is one representing a group of things (football team) or a member of a group of things (fullback). In the latter instance the concept is said to be *divisive*; in the former it is said to be *collective*. A precise concept is one quantified by a modifying constant. Precise concepts are of three kinds: 1) singular (the man, this woman, that child), 2) particular (some men, most women), 3) universal (all men, each man, every woman).

(c) On the basis of their mutual relations one with another, concepts may be classified as *apposite* and *opposite*.

Examples of apposite concepts are: chair, iron; bench, wood; government, democracy. Opposite concepts are themselves divided into four kinds: a) contradictory (organic, inorganic), b) contrary (red, blue), c) privative (sight, blindness), d) relative (husband, wife; student, teacher).

(d) On the basis of the degree of perfection of their representation, concepts may be classified as *clear* (atom, bomb) or *obscure* (atomic bomb, atomic energy). The subjectivity and consequent relativity that enters into this distinction is properly the concern of psychology. The logician, however, recognizes the existence of these two types of concepts.

SUPPLEMENTARY READINGS FOR CHAPTER II

Barnes, W. H. P., "The Doctrine of Connotation and Denotation," *Mind*, vol. 54, (July, 1945), pp. 254-263.

Burks, A. W., "Empiricism and Vagueness," *Journal of Philosophy*, vol. 43, (August, 1946), pp. 477-486.

Dunne, P., "The Production of the Intelligible Species," *The New Scholasticism*, vol. 27, (April, 1953), pp. 176-197.

Loewenberg, J., "The Futile Flight from Interpretation," *Meaning and Interpretation*, University of California Publications in Philosophy, vol. 25, 1950, pp. 169-197.

Murray, J., "The Platonic Doctrine of Ideas," *Studies*, vol. 40, 1951, pp. 311-322.

Peifer, J. F., *The Concept in Thomism*, Bookman Associates, New York, 1952.

Quine, W. V., "Identity, Ostension and Hypostasis," *Journal of Philosophy*, vol. 47, (October, 1950), pp. 621-633.

Sisson, E. O., "Things, Images, Ideas," *Journal of Philosophy*, vol. 45, (July, 1948), pp. 405-411.

Smith, G., "The Concept in St. Thomas," *The Modern Schoolman,* vol. 15, 1938, pp. 52-56.

Veatch, H. B., *Intentional Logic,* Yale University Press, New Haven, 1952, pp. 81-115.

CHAPTER III

The Sign of the Concept: The Term

The Sign

Necessity of Signs:

You may remember, from your childhood reading, the great joy that came to Robinson Crusoe when he found in Friday a companion for his loneliness. Man is by nature a social being. It is perhaps not far amiss to say that the need to communicate to others his thoughts and feelings is a need essential to man's very existence. There is perhaps no more convincing testament to this fact than the history of the poetry of the world's languages. "Conceptions of heart and mind come forth in silence and without sound, but by audible words the silence of the heart is manifested."[8] Man not only desires but needs to communicate, by means of sensible signs. Everywhere in the civilized world the practical manifestations of this need are in evidence; in banking, in commerce, in industry, in law, in medicine, in the classroom, and in the lecture hall. There is nothing that man does in his daily life (that in any way involves a relationship with another human intellect) which does not in some way have to do with sensible signs: signs of ideas, wishes, objects, etc. And it is one of the glories of his nature that, to satisfy this need which besets him on all sides, he is specially provided *by nature* with the physical means, to a degree of refinement beyond that of any other sentient organism.

Sign Defined:

Man communicates, we have said, by means of sensible signs; signs, that is to say, which are associated with his sensory apparatus. Speech sounds, says Aristotle, are the symbols of mental experiences; written words are the symbols of spoken ones.[9] A sign may be said to be that which *signifies* or gives significance to a thing; it is that which signifies to, or represents for, the intellect something other than itself. A sign is thus seen to be a two-fold thing: a) something in itself, and b) the bearer of a higher reality, its meaning or significance. A sign, further, involves a two-fold relation: first, to the object signified, for which it is a substitute; second, to an intellect capable of understanding.

Division of Signs:

Signs, like concepts, are of different kinds. The kinds of signs are distinguished from one another, first, on the basis of their relation to the objects they signify and, second, on the basis of their relation to the intellect which understands. In the first case, signs may be said to be *natural* or *artificial*. A natural sign is one which represents something distinct from itself by the very laws of nature and which bears to the object it signifies a *real* or natural relation. (Example: an infant's crying, as a sign of pain or discomfort.) An artificial sign is one which represents something distinct from itself by reason of public agreement, mutual consent, or convention and which bears to the object it signifies a *logical* relation. (Example: black, as a sign of death.) In the second case, signs may be said to be *instrumental* or *formal*. An instrumental sign is one which involves a recognition by the intellect, first, of the sign as a thing of and for itself, and second, of its relation to the object which it signifies or its referent — a double act of knowledge. Instrumental signs are themselves classified as a) natural, i.e. of the order of nature (smoke, as a sign of fire) and b) artificial, i.e. arbitrary or conventional (the flag, as the emblem of the nation). A formal sign is one which involves no recognition by the intellect of itself as a thing, but only the relation of the sign to its referent — a single act of knowledge. Formal signs are considered also to be natural ones. There are only two formal signs; these are the concept and the phantasm.

The Term Defined

A sign, now, is that which signifies to, or represents for, the mind an object or thing. The sign of the concept is called the term. A term may be defined as the written or spoken expression of a concept or idea. In speech, the term is an articulate sound or a series of sounds, associated by convention or custom with some fixed idea or meaning. In writing, the term is a syllable or group of syllables, associated likewise with a fixed idea or meaning. The term, both spoken or written, corresponds to what in language is called the *word*. By means of it man symbolizes and communicates his concepts.

Division of Terms

Terms, as signs of concepts, are divided according to their comprehension and extension in the same way that the concepts themselves are divided.[10] Terms are further classified, according to their exactness of signification, as univocal, equivocal, and analogical. A *univocal* term is one that signifies one thing and one thing only (gold, moon, oxygen). An *equivocal* term is one that signifies more than one thing, as in the case of a term which when spoken may signify one thing and when written another (dear, deer), or as in the case of a term which whether written or spoken may signify more than one thing (*bark*, as sound made by a dog or as covering of a tree). An *analogical* term is one that signifies two or more things among which exists a relationship of likeness (*foot*, as base of a mountain or part of the human body; *head,* as top-ranking officer or chief member of the human body).

A further division of terms is based on the grammar or structure of language. Grammar and logic, as we should begin to see now and as we shall see more and more, come together at many points. But with regard to the term, there frequently arises not a little confusion (and some increase in blood pressure) among rhetoricians and logicians. The problem of the reconcilement of terminology is, in reality, quite simple. The grammarian, as we know, divides the words of the language into *parts of speech,* in accordance with the way words function in the sentence, the basic unit of intelligible discourse. The logician classifies terms (i.e. words) as *variable* and *constant,* in accordance with the way they are used in the proposition, the basic unit of intelligible communication in logic. A variable term is one which may be removed from the proposition and replaced by another, of the same genus but different species, without destroying the integrity of the proposition. A constant term is one which may not be removed from the proposition and replaced by another without destroying the integrity of the proposition. Thus, in the proposition "*All* men *are* mortal," the terms in italics are constant, those not in italics are variable. One other thing, in addition, the logician does with the conventional divisioning of the grammarian. For him there are no verbs as such, other than the copula or linking verb *to be,* in all its forms. Thus: *John builds a house* becomes *John is building a house,* with the terms "John", "building", and "house" classified as variable and the others as constant. It becomes clear, then, that in logic all substantives (i.e. nouns, pronouns, and their like) and predicate adjectives (i.e. the adjective form of the subjective complement after linking or copulative verbs) are variables. The copula *to be* and all adverbs, simple adjectives, conjunctions, and prepositions are constants.

Properties of Terms

The term, again like the concept, has its special properties. A property, it will be remembered, is something that emerges or flows from a thing but is not the thing itself. With regard to terms, their properties are a consequence, as it were, of the fact that, while things (and hence concepts also) are unlimited in number, terms are limited in number. It is because of the inherent limitations of language that we have, for example, equivocal and analogical terms. Even if all terms were univocal, there still would be the problem of usage, i.e. the use of words in different contexts. It is thus inescapable that the same word or term may designate more than one thing or more than one aspect of things.

Out of this state of affairs, so to speak, comes what for the logician is the most consequential of the properties of the term — its *supposition*. The other properties of terms or words — called amplification, restriction, transfer, diminution, reimposition — are properly the concern of rhetoric and as such are not treated here. Supposition may be explained as the contextual use of a term, or the acceptance of a term as denoting something in a specific context. Its importance, from the viewpoint of logic, resides in its use for the verification of propositions. (Examples: *Lamb* is a word of one syllable. *Lamb* is a meat for human sustenance. He is the *Lamb* of God, Who takes away the sins of the world.) The supposition of a term is thus seen to be a thing distinct from its signification, the latter coming before the former. The signification is in, or belongs to, the word; but the supposition flows out of or emerges from the term, which is composed of the word and its signification. The manifold divisions that grow out of the property of supposition are seen in the diagram on the opposite page.

LOGIC OF DEFINITION

DIVISIONS OF SUPPOSITION

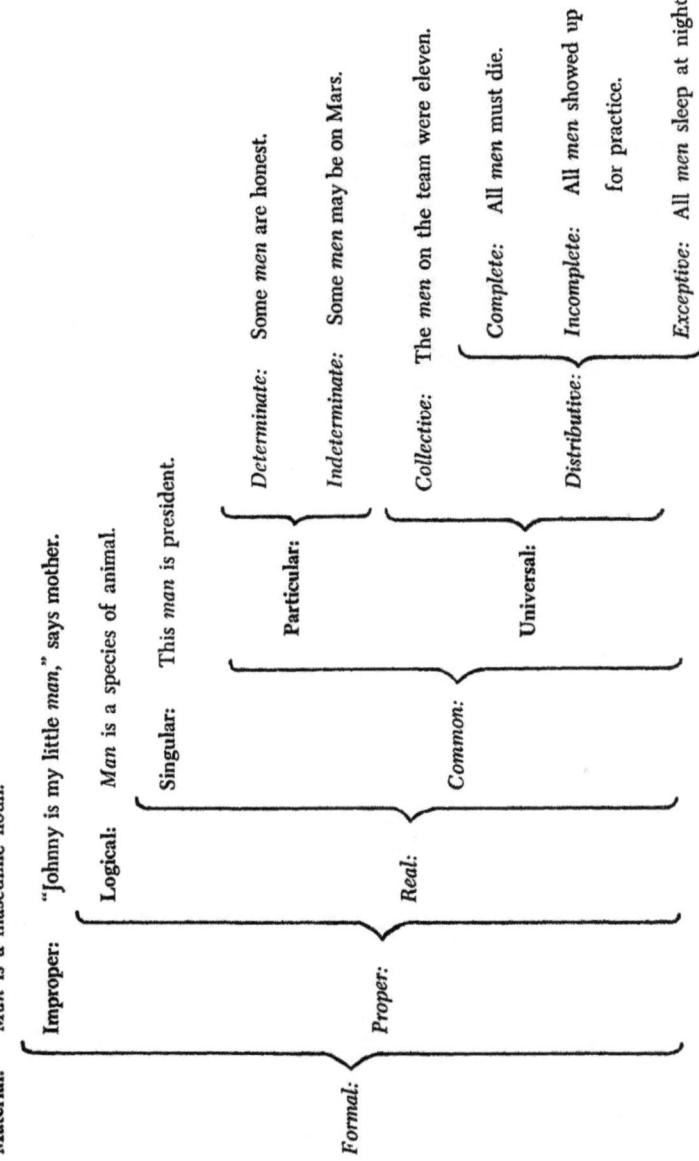

- **Material:** *Man* is a masculine noun.
- **Formal:**
  - **Improper:** "Johnny is my little *man*," says mother.
  - **Proper:**
    - **Logical:** *Man* is a species of animal.
    - **Real:**
      - **Singular:** This *man* is president.
      - **Common:**
        - **Particular:**
          - *Determinate:* Some *men* are honest.
          - *Indeterminate:* Some *men* may be on Mars.
        - **Universal:**
          - *Collective:* The *men* on the team were eleven.
          - *Distributive:*
            - *Complete:* All *men* must die.
            - *Incomplete:* All *men* showed up for practice.
            - *Exceptive:* All *men* sleep at night.

To the Student, an Exhortation

If you stop to think about it for a moment or two, out of the foregoing discussion of the sign and the term, of the kinds of signs and the kinds of terms, of the obvious relativity in the use of words there emerges an apparent need for caution and exactness in the choice of words for human discourse. The admonitions of the rhetorician — concerning the right word, concreteness, and economy of diction, concerning redundancy and circumlocution — add up, for the logician, to a single inclusive axiom, which might be worded as follows: *Always be careful in the use of terms; distinguish between the emotional and logical meanings of a term.*

SUPPLEMENTARY READINGS FOR CHAPTER III

Aldrich, V. C., "Language, Experience, and Pictorial Meaning," *Journal of Philosophy*, vol. 45, (February, 1948), pp. 85-95.

Aschenbrenner, K., "Intention and Understanding," *Meaning and Interpretation*, University of California Publications in Philosophy, vol. 25, 1950, pp. 229-270.

Ayer, A. J., *Language, Truth and Logic*, V. Gollancz, Ltd., London, 1936.

Ballard, E. S., "An Augustinian Doctrine of Signs," *The New Scholasticism*, vol. 23, 1949, pp. 207-211.

Basson, A. H., O'Connor, D. J., "Language and Philosophy," *Philosophy*, vol. 22, 1947, pp. 49-65.

Black, M., "A Symposium on Emotive Meaning," *The Philosophical Review*, vol. 57, 1948, pp. 111-126.

Boehner, P., "Ockham's Theory of Signification," *Franciscan Studies*, vol. 6, 1946, pp. 143-170.

————, "Ockham's Theory of Supposition and the Notion of Truth," *Franciscan Studies*, vol. 6, 1946, pp. 261-292.

————, *Medieval Logic*, The University of Chicago Press, Chicago, 1952, pp. 19-26.

————, *Medieval Logic*, The University of Chicago Press, Chicago, 1952, pp. 27-51.

Britton, K., *Communication, a Philosophical Study of Language,* Harcourt, Brace and Co., New York, 1939.

Brown, H. C., "The Use and Abuse of Language," *Journal of Philosophy,* vol. 26, (September, 1929), pp. 533-541.

Chase, S., *The Tyranny of Words,* Harcourt, Brace and Co., New York, 1937, pp. 226-243.

Dewey, J., "Peirce's Theory of Linguistic Signs, Thought, and Meaning," *Journal of Philosophy,* vol. 43, (February, 1946), pp. 85-95.

Flew, A. G. N., *Logic and Language,* The Philosophical Library, New York, 1951.

Foster, M. H., "Poetry and Emotive Meaning," *Journal of Philosophy,* vol. 47, (November, 1950), pp. 657-660.

Gentry, G., "Reference and Function," *Journal of Philosophy,* vol. 43, (January, 1946), pp. 37-47.

———, "Signs, Interpretants, and Significata," *Journal of Philosophy,* vol. 44, (June, 1947), pp. 318-324.

Gompetz, H., "The Meanings of 'Meaning'," *Philosophy of Science,* vol. 8, 1941, pp. 157-183.

Isenberg, A., "The Esthetic Function of Language," *Journal of Philosophy,* vol. 46, (January, 1949), pp. 5-20.

Johnson, A. B., *A Treatise on Language,* edited with critical essay, by David Rynin, University of California Press, Berkeley, 1947.

Kecskemeti, P., *Meaning, Communication, and Value,* The University of Chicago Press, Chicago, 1952, pp. 125-149.

Lachance, L., "The Philosophy of Language," *The Thomist,* vol. 4, 1942, pp. 547-588.

Lee, H. N., "The Use and Abuse of Words," *Journal of Philosophy,* vol. 39, (November, 1942), pp. 625-630.

McGill, V. J. "Notes on the Logic of Grammar," *The Philosophical Review,* vol. 39, 1930, pp. 459-478.

Meyer, J., "Language as a Biological Phenomenon," *Journal of Philosophy,* vol. 46, (June, 1949), pp. 387-393.

Moody, E. A., *The Logic of William of Ockham,* Sheed and Ward, New York, 1935, pp. 38-65.

Moore, W., "The Indexical and the Presentative Functions of Signs," *Philosophy of Science,* vol. 9, 1942, pp. 367-371.

Mullally, J. P., *The Summulae Logicales of Peter of Spain*, University of Notre Dame, Indiana, 1945, pp. 3-19.

O'Connor, D. J., "Philosophy and Ordinary Language," *Journal of Philosophy*, vol. 48, (December, 1951), pp. 797-808.

Oesterle, J. A., "The Problem of Meaning," *The Thomist*, vol. 6, 1943, pp. 180-229.

————, "Another Approach to the Problem of Meaning," *The Thomist*, vol. 7, 1944, pp. 233-263.

Ogden, C. K., and Richards, I. A., *The Meaning of Meaning*, Harcourt, Brace and Co., New York, 1936, pp. 1-23.

————, *The Meaning of Meaning*, Harcourt, Brace and Co., New York, 1936, Appendix C, pp. 266-290.

Quine, W. V., "Notes on Existence and Necessity," *Journal of Philosophy*, vol. 40, (March, 1953), pp. 113-115.

Richards, I. A., "A Symposium on Emotive Meaning," *The Philosophical Review*, vol. 57, 1948, pp. 145-157.

Stevenson, C. C., "A Symposium on Emotive Meaning," *The Philosophical Review*, vol. 57, 1948, pp. 127-144.

Veatch, H. B., *Intentional Logic*, Yale University Press, New Haven, 1952, pp. 10-28.

Weiner, P. P., "Philosophical, Scientific, and Ordinary Language," *Journal of Philosophy*, vol. 45, (May, 1948), pp. 260-266.

CHAPTER IV

Modes of Knowing Proper to the First Act

Why "Modes of Knowing"

So far, in the discussion of the concept and the term, we have of necessity stressed not *knowledge as a thing of itself* but rather the *mind's knowledge of knowledge.* That is to say, we have been concerned not with knowing what a being or an object is but with knowing that we know the being or object. It is one thing to know an object *as a pencil,* in the sense that we say of it, "This is a pencil"; it is another thing, however, to know *pencil,* in the sense that we say of it, "This is what a pencil is." In understanding an idea or a term, in reflecting upon it, in knowing it in its two-fold aspect of comprehension and extension, the mind must, of its nature, define and divide. Definition and division thus become, as will be seen below, mental forms or forms of knowledge by which the mind explains what it knows. Answering an inherent need of the intellect, they are its tools or implements, its *modes of knowing.* Through them, the intellect, in the act of apprehension, not only knows a *diamond* when it encounters one but also knows what the *diamond* is.

Definition

Definition Defined:

It is characteristic of the human mind that, when it apprehends a thing, it wants (as it were) to know it for what it is, to unfold its nature, to get at its meaning, to lay hold of what it comprehends (or includes) and what it extends to (or embraces). This unfolding of the nature of a thing, this getting at its meaning, this laying hold of what the thing comprehends and extends to is what is meant by *definition*. The word "define" comes from the Latin *de-finire*, which means "to state the limits of." To define a thing is thus to state its limits, to say *what it is,* and thus to imply what it is not. It is the mind's way of facing, so to speak, its own thoughts. You will do well to note, in passing, that to classify a thing (to say: "it is a pencil") is not to define; to designate or point out (to say: "this is a pencil") is likewise not to define.

Kinds of Definitions:

Definitions are classified as *nominal* (the term or word, i.e. the sign or name) and *real* (the signified or the thing itself). Nominal definitions are of two kinds: a) etymological (philosophy = love of wisdom) and b) vernacular (philosophy = view of life). Real definitions are also of two kinds: *intrinsic* and *extrinsic*.

Intrinsic definitions may be *essential* or *descriptive;* that is to say, they may have to do with the essences of things or with the contingencies of things. An essential definition may take the form of a statement of a) the proximate genus or class of a thing and b) the species or specific differences of a thing (man is a rational animal), in which case it is called a *metaphysical* definition. It may take the form of a statement of the natural elements of a thing (man is a creature composed of body and soul), in which case it is called a *physical* definition. A descriptive definition may take the form of a statement of the properties of a thing (man is a creature capable of laughing, weeping, smiling, scowling, etc.), and it is thus called proper. It may take the form of a statement of the accidents of a thing (man is a creature with two legs and ten toes), and it is thus called *accidental*.

Extrinsic definitions may be *genetic, exemplary,* or *ulterior;* that is to say, they may have to do with the origin or cause of a thing (man is a creature created by God), with the resemblance of a thing to some other thing (man is a creature made to the image and likeness of God), or with the purpose or end of a thing (man is a creature made to know, love, and serve God).

A Good Definition:

A good definition is one, quite simply, which is proper (i.e. appropriate or fitting) and exact (i.e. precise or accurate). The rules for a good definition might be said to be three. First: Make sure your definition is the kind you intend it to be. If you are intending to define a thing metaphysically, that is, by giving its proximate genus and species, then be sure you are defining it metaphysically and not physically, or etymologically, or genetically. Second: Make sure your definition is clear. Remember that the definition is a tool or implement, an aid or help to the mind; as such, its effectiveness depends upon its clarity. To define a thing in terms of its derivations ("definition is the process of defining") is not to be clear. To make a definition too inclusive ("Literature is writing") or too restrictive ("Chemistry is the study of atoms and molecules") is not to be clear. Third, and last: Make sure your definition is not a negative one, unless this is unavoidable. It is usually ineffective to define a thing in terms of what it is not. Negative definitions, nevertheless, are sometimes unavoidable. At times a definiendum (term to be defined) will require a negative definiens (defining term). Examples: "An invalid is a person who cannot walk." "A prime number is a number which cannot be divided."

The Division

Definition of Division:

The mind in laying hold of an object or thing, in getting at its meaning, in defining or analyzing it, follows a course or movement, so to speak, that in logic is called division. Division may be defined as the breaking down of a thing into its component parts or constituents. It is the designation of the species that constitute a genus. It is a statement of the component material elements of a thing. It is a compilation of the properties of a thing, of the notes of a concept, of the significations of a term.

Kinds of Division:

The breaking down of a term into its diverse significations constitutes a *nominal* division (pen = writing implement, play area for child, enclosure for pigs). The breaking down of an object or thing into its parts constitutes a *real* division. Real divisions are classified as *essential* or *accidental*.

An essential division may take the form of a breaking down of the natural elements of a thing (man = body + soul) in which case it is called a *physical* division. It may take the form of a breaking down of the notes of a concept or idea of a thing (man = corporeal, living, sentient, rational, etc.), in which case it is called a *metaphysical* division. It may take, further, the form of a breaking down of a genus into its proper species (man = men, women, children), in which case it is called a *logical* division.

An accidental division is a division of the accidents of a thing, i.e. of the attributes, aspects, etc. not essential but only accidental to the thing. Examples: *Man* = white men, black men, yellow men. *White* = milk-white, snow-white, egg-white.

A Good Division:

A good division is one which not only apparently but truly divides, or breaks down, a thing into its components or constituent parts. The rules governing a good division are more or less self-evident. First: there must be a *whole* capable of being divided. Since there is no indivisible thing (other than the Supreme Being, or God), this presents no problem. Second: there must be a principle (i.e. purpose or basis) of division. The concept *mankind* or *men*, for example, may be divided on any one of several bases or according to any one of several principles: age, size, color, nationality, etc. The term *literature*, again, may be divided on the basis of a) the kinds of literature, b) ages of literature, c) schools of literature, etc. Third: there must be a correspondence between the principle of division and the divided parts. Different principles of division result in different parts. *Mankind*, for example, cannot logically be divided into: white men, black men, Germans, pygmies. *Literature* cannot logically be divided into: poetry, neo-classical literature, essays, stream-of-consciousness fiction. Division, like definition, is an aid or help to the mind, an implement or tool. The difference between a good division and a poor one is not unlike the difference between a good tool and a poor one.

SUPPLEMENTARY READINGS FOR CHAPTER IV

Aristotle, *Topica*, 101b 39 - 103a 5.
Copilowish, I. M., "Border-line Cases, Vagueness, and Ambiguity," *Philosophy of Science*, vol. 6, 1939, pp. 181-195.
Dewey, J., Bentley, A. F., "Definition," *Journal of Philosophy*, vol. 44, (May, 1947), pp. 281-306.
Dubs, H. H., "Definition and Its Problems," *The Philosophical Review*, vol. 52, 1943, pp. 566-577.
Leblanc, H., "On Definitions," *Philosophy of Science*, vol. 17, 1950, pp. 302-309.
Ogden, C. K., Richards, I. A., *The Meaning of Meaning*, Harcourt, Brace and Co., New York, 1936, pp. 109-138.
Pepper, S. C., "The Descriptive Definition," *Journal of Philosophy*, vol. 43, (January, 1946), pp. 29-36.
Popkin, R., "The Function of Definitions in Social Science," *Journal of Philosophy*, vol. 40, (September, 1943), pp. 491-495.
Reid, J. R., "The Dilemma of Definition," *Journal of Philosophy*, vol. 36, (September, 1939), pp. 505-517.

Reid, J. R., "Definitional Rules: Their Nature, Status, and Normative Function," *Journal of Philosophy*, vol. 40, (April, 1943), pp. 188-192.

――――, "What are Definitions," *Philosophy of Science*, vol. 13, 1946, pp. 170-175.

Robinson, R., *Definition*, Oxford University Press, New York, 1950.

Ryan, J. K., "Verbal and Real Definitions," *Proceedings of the American Catholic Philosophical Association*, vol. 17, 1941, pp. 88-91.

Stevenson, C. L., "Persuasive Definitions," *Mind*, vol. 47, (July, 1938), pp. 331-350.

Toulmin, S. E., and Baier, K., "On Describing," *Mind*, vol. 61, (January, 1952), pp. 13-38.

FOOTNOTES TO PART ONE

1. *S.T.*, I a, q. 84, a. 7; J. of St. Thomas, *Cursus Phil.*, *Nat. Phil.* IV, q. 10, a. 3.
2. *S.T.*, I a, q. 76, a. 2; I a, q. 17, a. 3 ad lum.
3. See Introduction, p. 4.
4. Augustin Sesmat, *Logique*, vol. I, Hermann et Cie, Paris, 1950, p. 101.
5. Rudolph Allers, "On Intellectual Operations," *The New Scholasticism*, vol. 26, No. 1, 1952, pp. 21-36.
6. Sir William Hamilton, *Lectures on Logic*, i, W. Blackwood and Sons, Edinburgh and London, 1874-82, pp. 146 ff.
7. Some logicians fall into what the present writers consider to be the error of referring to the simple concept as a concept of a being having only one note — a thing impossible in the order of nature, if indeed even possible (except in the case of a Supreme Being) outside the natural order. It would seem illogical to consider a division of concepts on the basis of comprehension or wholeness without inferring a multiplicity of parts or notes. It is not possible to have a *whole* consisting of but one part. See, for example: C. N. Bittle, *The Science of Correct Thinking*, revised edition, Bruce, Milwaukee, 1951, p. 39.
8. Thomas Aquinas, Opusc. XIV, Expositio, *De Divinis Nominibus*, iv, lect. 1.
9. *De Interpretatione*, 16 a 4.
10. See Chap. II, p. 25.

Part Two

LOGIC
OF
PROPOSITIONS

The Second Act of the Mind

JUDGMENT

CHAPTER V

The Nature of the Act

Why the "Second" Act

Simple apprehension, now, involves the knowing of a thing, the awareness of it. A thing is apprehended when it is known for itself, independently of its relationship to or conformity with other things, independently of an inclination or need of the mind to affirm or deny anything about it beyond its mere existence or being. Of itself, apprehension, as we have seen, is an act of the mind which is incomplete and unsatisfactory. It is simple; it is indifferent to truth or falsity; it is static, because it neither affirms or denies. We have also seen it to be the first act of the mind because it is the one out of which the others grow and upon which they depend. It is, again, the point at which mental life begins.

The life of the mind, or intellectual knowledge, may not improperly be described as *generative* — in the sense that, like all generative things, it does not attain the fullness of itself all at once but attains it by degrees.[1] Though thought may move, so to speak, with a speed excelling that of the fastest-climbing rocket yet devised by modern technology, though your alarm clock may ring (let us carry the analogy to its wildest extremes) and you may read its face and climb out of bed with the speed of a Jim Thorpe, nevertheless thought is a progression, a series of steps, a moving from one point to the next. In the progression of intellectual knowledge, the first step or point is apprehension: the mind is aware of or knows things. The second step is judgment: the mind judges of what it knows.

The Psychology of Judgment

Within the progression of *acts of the mind*, which is the natural process of thought, there is yet an inner movement or sequence of steps, as it were. When the mind judges, three steps may be said to be involved in the act. First: the mind knows the things — and hence the terms and their proper uses — of which it is going to make a judgment. (The *foot* of the mountain is not the *foot* in your shoe.) Second: the mind establishes the identity or non-identity of things which it knows by relating them to and comparing them with other things which it likewise knows. (The *cultural heritage* of America is not as old as *that* of Britain.) Third: the mind gives its assent, indeed *agrees*, to the identity or non-identity of things; the mind *rests* in conviction or certainty. (Fred is a boy who can be trusted. Or: Fred *is not* a boy who can be trusted.)

The Judgment Defined

In the light of the psychology of the act and its relationship to and distinction from simple apprehension, the judgment may be defined as that act by which the mind assorts, separates, divides, or unites the things which it apprehends in order to establish their identity or non-identity for the ultimate purpose of affirming or denying their truth or falsity. It is that act, again, by which the mind is put at rest in conviction or certainty. Whereas apprehension is indifferent and static, judgment is assertive and dynamic; it answers the mind's need for satisfaction in certitude. Whereas the proper object of apprehension is the essence or quiddity of things, the proper object of the judgment is the existence or actuality of things. Thus, the one is essential, the other existential. Some prevailing synonyms for judgment are: synthesis, attribution, assent, interpretation, predication.

Components of Judgments

The judgment, we have just observed, is an assortment, separation, division, or union of apprehensions or concepts or things known. We see, then, that the components of a judgment are, simply, the mind's concepts or things known. The logician, however, in grouping concepts to arrive at judgments, makes yet another division of the parts of a judgment.

In the sentence, which in rhetoric is the counterpart of the stated judgment or proposition, we speak of two principal parts: the "subject" (that which is spoken of) and the "predicate" (that which is said of the subject). In logic, the judgment is said to consist of three principal parts. The first of these is the *subject:* a thing, a being, or an object of which something is affirmed or denied. (The *ship* is in the harbor. The *ship* is not in the harbor.) The second is the *copula* (all forms of the verb *to be* in the present tense in both the affirmative and the negative): the link by means of which we express the formal relation of the subject with that which is affirmed or denied of it. (The ship *is* in the harbor. The ship *is not* in the harbor.) The third is the *predicate:* that which is affirmed or denied of the subject. (The ship is *in the harbor.* The ship is not *in the harbor.*)

Predicates themselves, or predicaments, are further classified as *substantive* (substance) or *accidental* (accident). Substance (literally, that which "stands under") may be defined as that which exists in, of, and by itself; that is to say, the essence of a thing, its quiddity. A predicament is said to be substantive when it expresses the essence, the quiddity, or the substance of a thing. (The object seen in the harbor is a *ship.*) Accident (literally, that which is "added to") may be defined as that which exists in, of, and by another thing; that is to say, what is a part of but not necessary to something else.

There are nine classes of accidental predicaments. Predicaments may be:

a) *Quantitative:* expressive of the extension of a thing in space, its dimension. (The ship in the harbor is *a hundred feet long.*)

b) *Qualitative:* expressive of the qualities (i.e. habits and dispositions, capabilities, color, flavor, shape, etc.) of a thing. (The ship in the harbor is *a sleek white ship, built for speed.*)

c) *Relational:* expressive of the relationship of one thing to another, of the bearing of one thing upon another. (The ship in the harbor is a *ship of the Cunard Line.*)

d) *Active:* expressive of the action of one thing on another, of the production of one thing by another thing. (The ship in the harbor is *breaking all existing speed records.*)

e) *Passive:* expressive of the effect induced on a thing by another thing, of a reception by one thing of another. (The ship in the harbor is *being painted by the men.*)

f) *Temporal:* expressive of the existence of a thing in time or in a sequence of events. (The ship in the harbor is *five years old.*)

g) *Spatial:* expressive of the existence of a thing in space, of its relation to other things around it. (The ship in the harbor is *anchored to the right of the channel buoy.*)

h) *Positional:* expressive of the physical attitude of a thing, of the relative positions of its parts. (The ship in the harbor is *listing badly to starboard.*)

i) *Clothe-al:* expressive of the covering, the habiliment, the dress, or costume of a thing. (The ship in the harbor is *decked with flags.*)

The substantive predicate or predicament and the nine classes of accidental ones comprise what are called the *ten categories*. All predications about things must fall into one of these ten categories, which in themselves exhaust the possibilities of predication by the human mind. With them we may ask and answer all the questions that it is possible for the mind to ask and answer about things.

On the basis, now, of the number and kinds of components of the judgment, we may proceed further to a classification of the kinds of judgments, which are two: the *simple judgment* and the *complex judgment*. A simple judgment is one involving a single subject, a single copula, and a single predicate. (The ship is in the harbor.) A complex or compound judgment is one involving a plurality of subjects, or copulas, or predicates. (The ship is in the harbor but is not yet anchored.)

Properties of Judgments

The judgment, like the concept and its term, has its special properties. These may be considered to be two sets of related pairs rather than four distinct properties.

The first are *completeness* and *unity*. Completeness (allness or wholeness) and unity (oneness) characterize a judgment, whether simple or complex, when it really and not only apparently contains all its components (subject, copula, predicate) and when its components are logically related. Without completeness and unity there cannot be judgment, but only the semblance of judgment.

The second set of properties comprises *logical truth* and *logical falsity*. "What is truth?" was asked long before Pilate and has been asked many times since. Augustine of Hippo defined truth as "that whereby is made manifest that which is."[2] Thomas Aquinas defined truth as "the equation of thought and thing," and again as "the conformity of mind and thing."[3] On the basis of this, logical truth may be said to be the conformity or agreement between the mind and its objective evidence or that which is. Logical falsity may be said to be the disconformity or disagreement between the mind and its objective evidence or that which is.[4] In considering logical truth and falsity in connection with the judgment, let us add, it is important to keep in mind that the conformity or disconformity between the mind and its objective evidence is one thing, and a knowledge of the conformity or disconformity is another. To know the conformity or disconformity is to know truth fully. Not to know the conformity or disconformity, conversely, is not to know the truth fully. A judgment, then, is logically true and known to be logically true when it puts the mind at rest in the knowledge of the conformity between itself and what is.

A decade or more ago, when an ambitious advertising copy writer expressed on his typewriter the ambitious judgment: *More people smoke Ourkind than any other cigarette,* he was expressing a judgment which was *not complete* (because it started a comparison which it failed to finish), which *lacked unity* (because it compared people with cigarettes), which was *logically false* (because it expressed a disconformity between the mind and the thing), and which the copy writer *did not know* to be logically false (because he thought he was expressing the judgment that *People smoke more Ourkinds than any other cigarette*).

To the Student, a Clarification

It takes only a moment's thought to realize that, in the contemporary world in which we live, beset on all sides by newspapers, magazines, the radio, movies, and television, which have done more than their share in reducing public *thinking* to a minimum, a knowledge of the judgment as an act of the mind, of its *right uses*, is of incalculable importance. Only a fool, it was said earlier, would acknowledge himself in and satisfied with error. It is not enough to think we know what is, despite the fact that not only *More people smoke Ourkind than any other cigarette* but even, now, *More people buy Plymobiles than any other car!*

SUPPLEMENTARY READINGS FOR CHAPTER V

Aristotle, *Categoriae*, 1a-15b 33.

————, *Topica*, 103b 20 - 108b 32.

Boehner, P., "Ockham's Theory of Truth," *Franciscan Studies*, vol. 5, 1945, pp. 138-161.

Dewey, J., *Essays in Experimental Logic*, The University of Chicago Press, Chicago, 1916, pp. 230-249.

Geach, P. T., "Subject and Predicate," *Mind*, vol. 59, (October, 1950), pp. 461-482.

Hoenen, P., *Reality and Judgment According to St. Thomas*, Henry Regnery Co., Chicago, 1952, pp. 3-35.

————, *Reality and Judgment According to St. Thomas*, Henry Regnery Co., Chicago, 1952, pp. 36-72.

Kapp, E., *Greek Foundations of Traditional Logic*, Columbia University Press, New York, 1942, pp. 43-59.

Kaufmann, F., "Truth and Logic," *Philosophy and Phenomenological Research*, vol. 1, (September, 1940), pp. 59-69.

————, "Three Meanings of 'Truth'," *Journal of Philosophy*, vol. 45, (June, 1948), pp. 337-350.

Muller-Thym, B., "The To Be Which Signifies the Truth of Propositions," *Proceedings of the American Catholic Philosophical Association*, vol. 16, 1940, pp. 230-254.

Nagel, E., "Mr. Russell on Meaning and Truth," *Journal of Philosophy*, vol. 38, (May, 1941), pp. 253-270.

O'Toole, G. B., "Truth Is in the Judgment," *The New Scholasticism*, vol. 17, 1943, pp. 1-15.

Perkins, M., "Notes on the Pragmatic Theory of Truth," *Journal of Philosophy*, vol. 49, (August, 1952), pp. 573-587.

Sellars, R. W., "A Correspondence Theory of Truth," *Journal of Philosophy*, vol. 38, (November, 1941), pp. 645-654.

Sisson, E. O., "The Copula in Aristotle and Afterwards," *The Philosophical Review*, vol. 48, 1939, pp. 57-64.

Smith, G., "Note on Predication," *The New Scholasticism*, vol. 15, 1941, pp. 222-237.

Tarski, A., "The Semantic Conception of Truth," *Readings in Philosophical Analysis*, Appleton-Century-Crofts, New York, 1949, pp. 52-84.

Thayer, H. S., "Two Theories of Truth: The Relation between the Theories of John Dewey and Bertrand Russell," *Journal of Philosophy*, vol. 44, (September, 1947), pp. 516-527.

Thomas Aquinas, *Truth*, Translated by R. Mulligan, S.J., Henry Regnery Co., Chicago, 1952, vol. I, pp. 3-51.

Thompson, M. H., "J. S. Mill's Theory of Truth," *The Philosophical Review*, vol. 56, 1947, pp. 273-292.

Toohey, J. J., "Proposition, Judgment, and Inference," *Journal of Philosophy*, vol. 37, (April, 1940), pp. 232-243.

Tyrrell, F. M., "Concerning the Nature and Function of the Act of Judgment," *The New Scholasticism*, vol. 26, (October, 1952), pp. 393-423.

CHAPTER VI

The Internal Product of the Act: The Mental Statement

The Mental Statement Defined

Whereas the end product of the act of apprehension is the concept or mental word, the end product of the judgment is its mental statement. Like the concept, the mental statement is a product in the sense that it is something the mind forms; it is internal in the sense that it is formed within the mind. The mental statement may be defined as the representation formed in and by the mind, when the mind assorts, separates, divides, or unites concepts, that is say, when the mind synthesizes, attributes, assents, interprets, predicates. Let it be noted that the mental statement is a thing that may be considered in, of, and by itself. Let it also be noted that the mental statement and the mind which forms it are distinct things. The certitude of a mental statement resides not merely in the truth of the mental statement, but in the mind's knowledge of the truth of the mental statement.

Components of Mental Statements

The components of a mental statement may be described on the one hand as *material* and on the other hand as *formal*. The concepts or mental words which are separated or united, the subject and predicate, in other words, constitute the "matter" of the mental statement. The union or separation, the composition or division, the inclusion or exclusion (signified by the copula, *is* or *is not*) determines the *form* of the mental statement.

The Rôle of the Mental Statement

Logic, as we have noted earlier, may not improperly be defined as the ordering of our thoughts. Our thoughts, of course, are our concepts. The concept, we know, is the point at which our mental life begins. Nevertheless, thought, considered in the abstract, that is to say thinking, may be said to begin with the ordering of our concepts, or with judgment. The mental statement, which is the representation to the mind of its judgments, is the point at which logic may be said truly to begin. Here, now, is thinking. Here is the mind, in one sense knowing, but in another sense working, ordering, exercising logic.

CHAPTER VII

The Sign of the Mental Statement: The Proposition

The Proposition Defined

The sign of the mental statement is called the proposition. The proposition may be defined as the written or spoken expression of a mental statement. The proposition is the basic unit of intelligible logical communication. In rhetoric it has its counterpart, as we have seen, in the sentence. It is the point at which logic moves outward, from the mind, to what is outside the mind.

Components of Propositions

If the components of the judgment are the concepts which the mind groups, divides, and unites, then the components of the proposition are the terms or words signifying the concepts so grouped, divided, or united. We have already seen[5] that terms or words are classified in logic, in accordance with the way they are used by the mind, as constant or variable. We have also seen that, in logic, all substantives (nouns, pronouns, and their like) and predicate adjectives (the adjective form of the subjective complement after linking or copulative verbs) are variables; and that the copula *to be* and all adverbs, simple adjectives, conjunctions, and prepositions are constants. All propositions may thus be said to consist of variable terms whose comprehensive and extension are affected by modifying constants. Terms, then, constitute the material or "matter" of the proposition. The terms which correspond to the subject and predicate of the mental statement of which the proposition is an expression are referred to as the *extremes* (term = terminus) of the proposition. The term which corresponds to the copula of the mental statement, by uniting or dividing the extremes of the proposition, determines, explicitly or implicitly, its "form".

In the case of the *uniting* by the copula of the extremes, in a true affirmative proposition (*The whale is a mammal*) it is to be noted that the subject and the predicate signify the same thing in reality but different things in idea. This is true whether the predicate be a substantive one or an accidental one. To say *The whale is black* is to identify "whaleness" and "blackness" in the object or being, while at the same time recognizing that "whaleness" and "blackness" are different in idea. In a proposition in which a thing is predicated of itself (*The earth is the earth*) the same holds true. Here, the subject and predicate are identified in reality but are different things in idea, inasmuch as the subject "earth" represents to the mind the individual *substance* (the object or being) whereas the predicate "earth" represents to the mind the *form* (idea). It is because, in this sense, subjects are taken *materially* and predicates *formally*, that, though the mind unites or composes the subject and predicate in a relationship of identity, it recognizes at the same time their diversity in, or plurality of, idea.[6]

Division of Propositions

Propositions are divided one from another according to five principles of division: a) unity, b) quality, c) quantity, d) time, e) matter.

(a) On the basis of unity, propositions are classified as *simple* or *complex*. A simple proposition, like the simple judgment of which it is the outward expression, is one consisting of a single subject, a single copula, and a single predicate. Conversely, the complex proposition is one consisting of a multiplicity of subjects or copulas or predicates. A proposition may be explicitly complex, when it includes any one of the conjunctions of the language (*and, but, or, nor, either, neither, if, because,* etc.) or a preposition substituting for a conjunction in a grammatical ellipsis, as in: The whale is a mammal *but* the shark is not; or, The whale *and* the shark live in the sea; or, *Neither* the whale *nor* the shark is found in lakes; or, All the nations coöperate *except* Russia. A proposition may be implicitly complex, when one or more of the terms is affected by a grammatical modifier (an adjective, an adverb), as in: Among sea creatures the whale *alone* is a mammal; or, *Only* Russia does not coöperate; or, Even a fool is *sometimes* right by chance.

(b) On the basis of the quality of the copula, propositions are classified as *categorical* or *modal*. Categorical propositions are of two kinds. When the extremes of the proposition are linked by the copula *is*, the proposition is said to be an *affirmative* one. (The whale *is* a mammal); when they are linked by the copula *is not*, the proposition is said to be a *negative* one (The shark *is not* a mammal). Modal propositions are of four kinds. When the copula expresses a relationship, between the subject and predicate, of possibility (Even a fool *can* be right by chance), the proposition is called a *possible* one. When the copula expresses a relationship of impossibility (A blind man *cannot* see), the proposition is called an *impossible* one. When the copula expresses a relationship of contingency or accidence (A blind man *may* be cured of his affliction), the proposition is called a *contingent* or *accidental* one. When the copula expresses a relationship of necessity (All men *must* die), the proposition is called a *necessary* or *essential* one.

(c) On the basis of the quantity or extension of the subject term, propositions are classified as *indefinite* or *definite*. An indefinite proposition is one whose subject, whether abstract or concrete, is not quantified by a modifying constant (*Pride* goeth before a fall) (*Boys* will be boys). A definite proposition is one whose subject is quantified by a modifying constant. Definite propositions are themselves of three kinds: *singular* (*This* house is not a barn), *particular* (*Some* houses are not barns), *universal* (*No* house is a barn).

(d) On the basis of time, or the grammatical tense expressed by the copula, propositions are classified as: *present* (The house *is* mine), *past* (The house *was* mine), *future* (The house *will be* mine).

(e) On the basis of matter, or the "material" of which they are constituted, propositions are classified as *impossible*, *contingent*, or *necessary*. An impossible proposition is one whose extremes are illogically related by the copula, and in this sense cannot be so related by the copula in question; that is to say, the predicate is not found within the comprehension of the subject (A dog is a man, A hat is a shoe, etc.). A contingent proposition is one whose extremes may, but need not, be related by the copula; that is to say, the predicate may, but need not, be found within the comprehension of the subject (The chair is made of wrought iron, The sky is overcast with clouds, etc.). A necessary proposition is one whose extremes must, necessarily, be related by the copula; that is to say, the predicate must always be found within the comprehension of the subject (All men will some day die, Wood burns in the fire, etc.).

Classification of Propositions into "A", "E", "I", "O"

When we integrate *quality* and *quantity*, in the case of propositions, another classification suggests itself. When propositions occur in numbers, as they do when the mind thinks and when one mind communicates its thought to another, it becomes practical for the logician, in order to facilitate his discussion of them, to classify propositions into four inclusive groups identified by the arbitrary symbols *A*, *E*, *I*, and *O* as follows:

- *A*: standing for *universal affirmative propositions* (All whales are mammals),

- *E*: standing for *universal negative propositions* (Sharks are not mammals; i.e., No sharks are mammals),

- *I*: standing for *particular affirmative propositions* (Some mammals are whales),

- *O*: standing for *particular negative propositions* (Some mammals are not whales).

In bringing these inclusive classes to the proposition as we now know it, let us note several things. First: *singular* propositions behave like universal ones (*A* or *E*). Second: *indefinite* propositions with a concrete subject term may be universal or particular (*A*, *E*, *I*, or *O*). Third: *indefinite* propositions with an abstract subject term are universals (*A* or *E*). Fourth: *modal* propositions of *necessity* are universal affirmatives (*A*); modal propositions of *impossibility* are universal negatives (*E*); modal propositions of *contingency* and *possibility* when affirmative are particular affirmatives (*I*), and when negative are particular negatives (*O*).[7]

When we further integrate *quality*, *quantity*, and *matter* in the case of propositions, still another classification suggests itself. Disregarding the proposition in impossible matter (since there is no point in discussing the impossible), and concerning ourselves with propositions in necessary matter and contingent matter, we may make a further distinction among propositions, as being *N* (necessary matter) or *C* (contingent matter). Thus a given proposition may be classified not merely as *A, E, I,* or *O,* but also as *AC, AN, EC, EN,* etc.

Logical Relations of Propositions

When we further integrate quality, quantity, and matter with the two most generic or inclusive properties of all propositions (as they are of judgments), *truth* and *falsity,* we arrive at important distinctions among the various logical relations that propositions may have one with another. By logical relation, now, is meant the bearing that one proposition may have upon another when the terms of the propositions are the same ones or relevant ones. (Examples: No barns are red. Some barns are red. All barns are red. Not all barns are red.) The kinds of relations that exist among relevant or interrelated propositions are three, called: *opposition, conversion, obversion.*

Opposition:

Logical opposition may be defined as the successive affirmation and negation (denial) of identical predicates of identical subjects (The book is here. The book is not here). Let it be noted that three conditions, so to speak, must prevail if we are to have an actual instance of logical opposition. One: the propositions must have the same extremes, that is, the same subject and the same predicate. Two: the terms of the proposition (variables and constants), where the same, must have the same signification or meaning and the same supposition. Three: the copulas of the propositions must be *opposite* in quality (*is, is not; can, cannot; may, may not; must, must not*).

There are four varieties of logical opposition which may be met with when two propositions are related. These are:

(a) *Opposition of contradiction.* By this is meant the opposition of propositions, one of which purely and simply denies what the other affirms. This type of opposition occurs when *A* and *O* propositions are related, or when *E* and *I* propositions are related, or when, in the case of two singular propositions, one denies the other. The following rule emerges out of the foregoing: Two contradictory propositions, whether in necessary or contingent matter, cannot be at the same time true or at the same time false.

(b) *Opposition of contrariety.* By this is meant the opposition of propositions which cannot be true together but can be false together. This type occurs when *A* and *E* propositions are related. Again a rule: Two contrary propositions, in necessary or contingent matter, opposed in quality but not in quantity, cannot be true together. In contingent matter, however, if one is false the other may also be false.

(c) *Opposition of sub-contrariety.* By this is meant the opposition of propositions which cannot be false together but can be true together at the same time. This occurs when *I* and *O* propositions are related. And the rule: Two sub-contrary propositions, in necessary or contingent matter, opposed in quality but not in quantity, do not negate (deny) or exclude each other; rather, one would deny what a third, more extended proposition would affirm. (Example: Some food is eaten, Some food is not eaten. All food is eaten.) This is explained by reason of the fact that, if two sub-contraries were false at the same time, their contradictories would be true at the same time; and, since these contradictories are themselves contraries, we would seem to have the impossible instance of two contrary propositions being true simultaneously. As an extension of this, note that, in necessary and contingent matter, if one is false the other is true; in contingent matter, if one is true the other may also be true.

(d) *Opposition of subalternation.* In this case, we have what is not truly a logical opposition but rather a relation between superior and inferior propositions, this is to say between a proposition that is universal and one that is particular. This type of "opposition" occurs when *A* and *I* propositions are related and when *E* and *O* propositions are related. The rule in this case: In necessary or contingent matter, if the universal proposition is true the particular is true, if the particular is false the universal is false. In necessary matter, if the universal is false the particular is false, but, in contingent matter, if the universal is false the particular is true.

All the relationships of opposition which propositions may have one with another are shown in the diagrams on the following pages.

Conversion:

Logical conversion may be defined as the inverting or interchanging of the extremes of a proposition (that is, putting the subject in the position of the predicate and vice versa) in such a way as to restate or express the same truth. (Example: Some barns are red. Some red things are barns.) The conversion of a proposition is to be distinguished from the perversion of a proposition. If the inverting of the extremes of a proposition destroys the truth of the proposition, the proposition is said to be perverted rather than converted. (Example: All whales are mammals. All mammals are whales.) There are three kinds of logical conversion. These are:

(a) *Simple conversion.* By this is meant the interchanging of the extremes without changing the quantity of the original proposition. (Example: Some men are public officials. Some public officials are men.)

(b) *Accidental conversion.* By this is meant the interchanging of the extremes together with the changing of the quantity of the original proposition. (Example: All men are animals. Some animals are men.)

(c) *Contrapositional conversion.* By this is meant the interchanging of the extremes together with the adding of

LOGIC OF PROPOSITIONS

SQUARE OF OPPOSITION OF CATEGORICAL PROPOSITIONS

(A) In necessary Matter

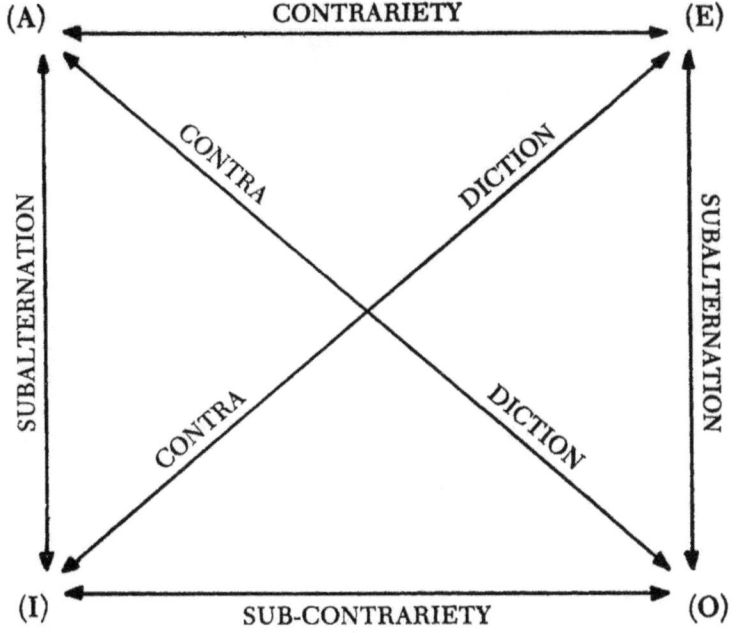

(B) In Contingent Matter

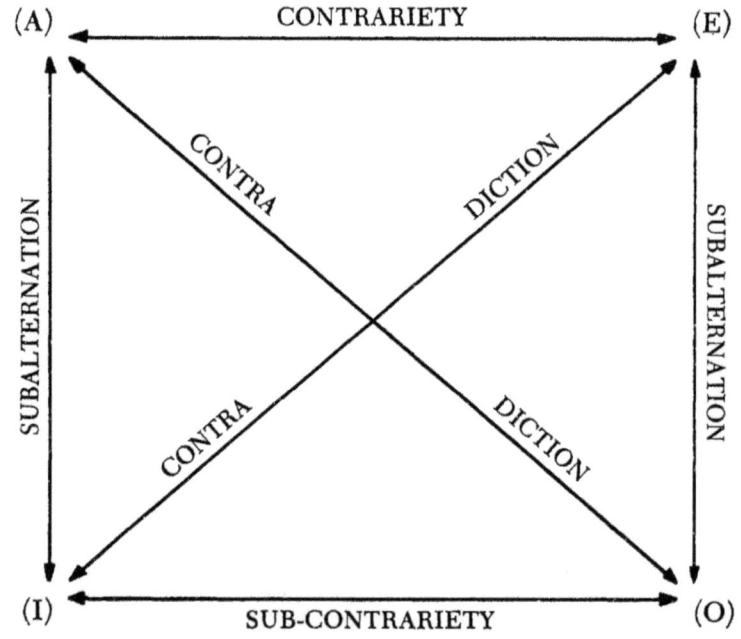

SQUARE OF OPPOSITION OF MODAL PROPOSITIONS

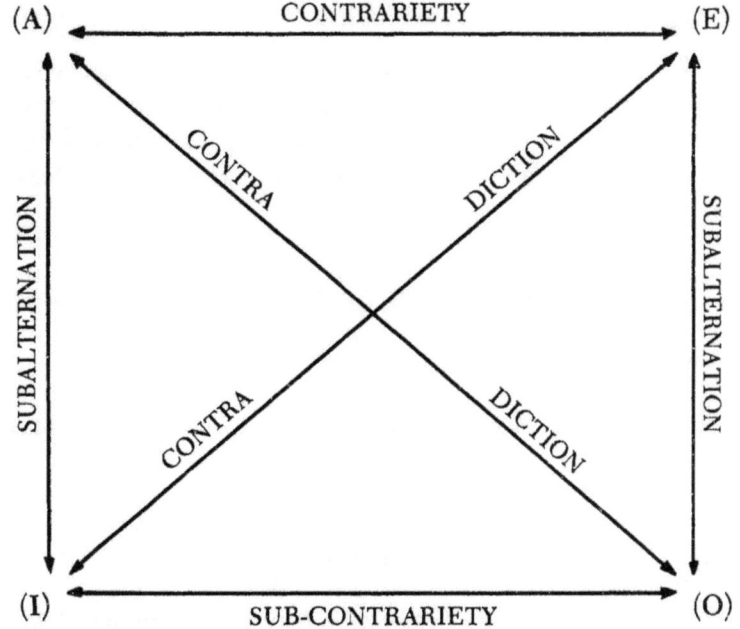

a negative particle to the interchanged subject and predicate, without changing the quantity of the original proposition. (Example: The Chinese are kind people. Unkind people are not Chinese.)

The following rules, now emerge out of the foregoing:

1) A propositions are never converted simply but always accidentally.
2) E and I propositions are always converted simply.
3) O propositions can never be converted.

Obversion:

Logical obversion or equivalence may be defined as the equating or bringing together in agreement two opposed propositions, by adding a negative particle to one of them. (Example: Some men are kind; some men are unkind. Some men are not unkind.)

SUPPLEMENTARY READINGS FOR CHAPTER VII

Adler, M., *Dialectic*, Harcourt, Brace and Company, New York, 1927, pp. 142-199.

Aldrich, V. C., "Do Commands Express Propositions?" *Journal of Philosophy*, vol. 40, (November, 1943), pp. 654-657.

Aristotle, *De Interpretatione*, 16a 1-24b 14.

———, *Topica*, 128b 14 - 139a 20.

Baylis, C. A., "Are Some Propositions Neither True Nor False?" *Philosophy of Science*, vol. 3, 1936, pp. 156-166.

Beardsley, E. L., "The Semantical Aspect of Sentences," *Journal of Philosophy*, vol. 40, (July, 1943), pp. 393-403.

Bisbee, E., "Confusion About Exclusive and Exceptive Propositions," *The Philosophical Review*, vol. 46, 1937, pp. 85-88.

Black, M., "The Analysis of a Simple Necessary Statement," *Journal of Philosophy*, vol. 40, (January, 1943), pp. 39-46.

Brown, R., and Watling, J., "Counterfactual Conditionals," *Mind*, vol. 61, (April, 1952), pp. 222-233.

Clark, J. T., *Conventional Logic and Modern Logic*, Woodstock College Press, Woodstock, Md., 1952, pp. 35-59.
Collins, J., "Mr. Lewis and the A Priori," *Journal of Philosophy*, vol. 45, (October, 1948), pp. 561-572.
Copleston, F. C., "A Note on Verification," *Mind*, vol. 59, (October, 1950), pp. 522-529.
Dewey, J., "Propositions Warranted Assertibility, and Truth," *Journal of Philosophy*, vol. 38, (March, 1941), pp. 169-186.
Doyle, J. J., "In Defense of the Square of Opposition," *The New Scholasticism*, vol. 25, 1951, pp. 367-396.
————, "The Hexagon of Relationships," *The Modern Schoolman*, vol. 29, No. 2, 1952, pp. 93-97.
————, "John of St. Thomas and Mathematical Logic," *The New Scholasticism*, vol. 27, (January, 1953), pp. 2-38.
Ducasse, C. J., "Propositions, Opinions, Sentences, and Facts," *Journal of Philosophy*, vol. 37, (December, 1940), pp. 701-711.
————, "Truth, Verifiability, and Propositions about the Future," *Philosophy of Science*, vol. 8, 1941, pp. 329-337.
Edwards, P., "Necessary Propositions and the Future," *Journal of Philosophy*, vol. 46, (March, 1949), pp. 155-156.
————, "Do Necessary Propositions 'Mean Nothing'?" *Journal of Philosophy*, vol. 46, (July, 1949), pp. 457-468.
Eslick, L. J., "Grammatical and Logical Forms," *The New Scholasticism*, vol. 13, 1939, pp. 233-244.
Goodman, N., "The Problem of Conterfactual Conditions," *Journal of Philosophy*, vol. 44, (February, 1947), pp. 113-128.
Greenwood, T., "The Metaphysical Ground of Logical Operations," *The New Scholasticism*, vol. 16, 1942, pp. 150-166.
Hoenen, P., *Reality and Judgment According to St. Thomas*, Henry Regnery Co., Chicago, 1952, pp. 73-94.
————, *Reality and Judgment According to St. Thomas*, Henry Regnery Co., Chicago, 1952, pp. 95-133.
Jacoby, P., "A Triangle of Opposites for Types of Propositions in Aristotelian Logic," *The New Scholasticism*, vol. 24, 1950, pp. 32-56.
Kaplan, A., Copilowish, I. M., "Must There Be Propositions?" *Mind*, vol. 48, (October, 1939), pp. 478-484.

Markenke, P., "Propositions and Sentences," *Meaning and Interpretation*, University of California Publications in Philosophy, vol. 25, 1950, pp. 273-298.

Newman, J. H., *A Grammar of Assent*, The Catholic Publication Society, New York, 1870, pp. 17-33.

Oliver, W. D., "Logic and Necessity," *Journal of Philosophy*, vol. 47, (February, 1950), pp. 69-73.

Quine, W. V., "Notes on Existence and Necessity," *Journal of Philosophy*, vol. 40, (March, 1943), pp. 113-127.

————, "On the Logic of Quantification," *Journal of Symbolic Logic*, vol. 10, 1945, pp. 1-12.

————, "The Problem of Interpreting Modal Logic," *Journal of Symbolic Logic*, vol. 12, 1947, pp. 43-48.

Ross, A., "Imperatives and Logic," *Philosophy of Science*, vol. 11, 1944, pp. 30-46.

Russell, B., "On Denoting," *Readings in Philosophical Analysis*, Appleton-Century-Crofts, Inc., New York, 1949, pp. 103-115.

Sheldon, W. H., "Necessary Truths and the Necessary Being," *Journal of Philosophy*, vol. 26, (April, 1929), pp. 197-209.

Smith, H. B., "Meaning," *Journal of Philosophy*, vol. 26, (March, 1929), pp. 182-185.

Spaulding, E. G., "Are There Any Necessary Truths?" *Journal of Philosophy*, vol. 26, (June, 1929), pp. 309-329.

Tallon, H. J., "Russell's Doctrine of the Logical Proposition," *The New Scholasticism*, vol. 13, 1939, pp. 31-48.

Thompson M. H., "On Aristotle's Square of Opposition," *The Philosophical Review*, vol. 62, (April, 1953), pp. 251-65.

Veatch, H., "Basic Confusions in Current Notions of Propositional Calculi," *The Thomist*, vol. 14, 1951, pp. 238-258.

————, *Intentional Logic*, Yale University Press, New Haven, 1952, pp. 154-188.

————, *Intentional Logic*, Yale University Press, New Haven, 1952, pp. 331-344.

Walton, W. M., "The Second Mode of Necessary or Per Se Propositions According to St. Thomas Aquinas," *The Modern Schoolman*, vol. 29, No. 4, 1952, pp. 293-306.

Weinberg, J. R., "Contrary-to-Fact Conditionals," *Journal of Philosophy*, vol. 48, (January, 1951), pp. 17-22.

CHAPTER VIII

Mode of Knowing Proper to the Second Act

Immediate Inference

Definition and division, we have seen, are the modes of knowing proper to simple apprehension, the first act of the mind. Answering an inherent need of the intellect, they are mental forms or forms of knowledge by which the mind explains what it knows. The mode of knowing proper to the second act of the mind is called *immediate inference*. It, too, is a tool or implement, inherent in the intellect.

The life of the intellect, we have already begun to see, involves a *moving* (as it were) of the mind from one idea to another, from one judgment to another. The path or the course or the direction which the mind takes in moving from one judgment to another or to others is given the general name of *inference*. As a generic term inference may be regarded as synonymous with consequence, implication, inclusion, suggestion. It is, in a sense, the mind's awareness of a judgment (and hence of a proposition) not in isolation but in its natural relation to other relevant judgments (and hence propositions). Beginning with a judgment or judgments, in other words, the mind arrives at another judgment, or conclusion, the logical truth or falsity of which is a consequence of, is implied in, is included in, is suggested by that of the others. There are two kinds of inference, immediate and mediate. A mediate inference is an inference drawn from more than one judgment, that is, one that grows out of the inter-relationship of two or more given judgments. It is proper to the third act of the mind and will be discussed in Part Three.

An immediate inference is one drawn directly from a single proposition. It is, simply, the act of passing from one judgment to another, hence from one proposition to another. It is a kind of "criticism" or "testing" of the original judgment or proposition. It is the mind's way of arriving immediately at what is the consequence of, what is implied or included in, what is suggested by a single, given judgment or proposition.

Kinds of Immediate Inference

The kinds of immediate inference, a moment's reflection will show, correspond to the kinds of logical relations that exist between propositions. These will be recalled as, one: *opposition*, of which there are four varieties, opposition of contradiction, of contrariety, of sub-contrariety, and of subalteration; two: *conversion*, of which there are three varieties, simple, accidental, and contrapositional; three: *obversion*. A re-examination of the examples given to illustrate these logical relations will make clear the kinds of immediate inference the mind can make.

Utility of Immediate Inference

Inference, as was said, is inherent in the intellect; it is natural to the mind; it is, so to speak, the mind's way of functioning. Without immediate inference the mind would be frozen in a state of intellectual inertia; without it rational existence as we know it would be impossible. The more practical consequences of immediate inference, also, are apparent. To know what we are saying, what others are saying, what the real implications of a statement are, how legal documents (like our constitution and the public laws) are to be interpreted, we rely on inference. Immediate inference is the means by which we know an expressed judgment as a unit of intelligible communication, by which we know its import, along with its bearings, its limits, its full logical contextual intention and extension.

To the Student, an Application

It would seem appropriate at this point to alert ourselves against what are called *propositional fallacies,* which invariably are the result of incorrect, subjective, or dishonest inferences. A propositional fallacy may take the form of a constructional ambiguity, as in the case of a proposition which is incomplete and lacking unity (*More people buy Plymobiles than any other car*). It may take the form of a faulty conversion, as when an attempt is made to convert an A proposition simply (*All taxes are forms of revenue* to *All forms of revenue are taxes*). It may take the form of a shift in accent, as when an attempt is made to suggest a judgment without being held responsible for it (*Yes, I said he's dishonest, that's true* to *Yes, I said he's dishonest; THAT'S true*). It may take the form of an *ad hominem* (name calling) proposition: *Because he is a liar, nothing he says may be believed.* It may take the form of an *ad verecundiam* (glittering generalization) proposition: *Every decent, God-fearing American cannot think otherwise.* It may take the form of an *ad populum* (popular appeal) proposition: *Everybody's doing it; why don't you?*

A proposition, then, let it be noted, is a good proposition when its terms are clear and logically related, when it has unity and completeness, when the immediate inferences drawn from it are correct ones, objective ones, and honest ones.

SUPPLEMENTARY READINGS FOR CHAPTER VIII

Bakan, M. B., "Logical Inference and Being," *Journal of Philosophy*, vol. 49, (November, 1952), pp. 713-722.

Hiz, H., "On the Inferential Sense of Contrary-to-Fact Conditionals," *Journal of Philosophy*, vol. 48, (September, 1951), pp. 586-587.

Lafleur, L. J., "The Fluxive Fallacy," *Philosophy of Science*, vol. 7, 1940, pp. 92-96.

Minogue, G. P., "Immediate Inrefences: Are They Really Inferences?" *The New Scholasticism*, vol. 18, 1944, pp. 284-292.

Newman, J. H., *A Grammar of Assent*, The Catholic Publication Society, New York, 1870, pp. 248-329.

————, *A Grammar of Assent*, The Catholic Publication Society, New York, 1870, pp. 330-372.

Richards, I. A., *How to Read a Page*, W. W. Norton & Co., Inc., New York, 1942.

Sidwick, A., *Fallacies*, Kegan Paul, Trench, Tröbner & Co., Ltd., London, 1901.

Smith, H. B., *How the Mind Falls into Error*, Harpers & Brothers, New York, 1923.

Stebbing,* L. S., *Thinking to Some Purpose*, Penguin Books, New York, 1939.

Walsh, F. A., "An Introductory Study of Error and Fallacies," *The New Scholasticism*, vol. 1, 1927, pp. 333-342.

Wellmuth, J., "Two Views on Immediate Inference," *The New Scholasticism*, vol. 18, 1944, pp. 123-146.

FOOTNOTES TO PART TWO

1. *S.T.*, I a, q. 85, a. 5.
2. *De Vera Religione*, XXXVI.
3. *S.T.*, I a, q. 16, a. 1 and a. 2.
4. "The fact of the being of a man carries with it the truth of the proposition that he is, and the implication is reciprocal: for if a man is, the proposition wherein we allege that he is is true, and conversely, if the proposition wherein we allege that he is is true, then he is. The true proposition, however, is in no way

the cause of the being of the man, but the fact of the man's being does seem somehow to be the cause of the truth of the proposition, for the truth or falsity of the proposition depends on the fact of the man's being or not being." Aristotle, *Categoriae*, 14b 14 - 14b 22.
5. Chapter III, p. 31 ff.
6. *S.T.*, I a, q. 13, a. 12.
7. Some confusion exists among logicians as to the classification of modal propositions of *contingency* in the A, E, I, O scheme. In consideration of the interrelationship between the contingent and the possible (between what *can* be and what *may* be), the view of the writers coincides with the view of those who hold that contingent propositions are to be classified (like possible propositions) as I or O, depending upon whether they are affirmative or negative, and not only as O. See, for example, Jacques Maritain, *Formal Logic*, Sheed and Ward, New York, 1946, p. 138; Raymond J. McCall, *Basic Logic*, Barnes and Noble, New York, 1947, p. 79.

Part Three

LOGIC OF ARGUMENTATION

The Third Act of the Mind

REASONING

CHAPTER IX

The Nature of the Act

The Psychology of Reasoning

Thought begins, we have seen, with apprehension; it begins with the mind's attaining concepts, by means of which the mind knows what is outside itself. It proceeds thence to judgment, which is the act by which the mind groups and arranges objective concepts in order to establish their identity or non-identity for the ultimate purpose of affirming or denying their truth or falsity. By means of immediate inference, further, the mind builds upon its judgments, arrives at other judgments which are relevant to or grow out of the judgments it already has. If thought were to stop here, it would still be in the natural order a phenomenon of marvelous import, a faculty to place man in his nature above every other sentient organism on the earth. But thought, of course, does not stop here.

When the mind judges, again, it answers for itself an inherent need to be put at rest in conviction or certainty. It is not enough to have concepts; the mind must verify them for itself, must affirm for itself their truth. But out of judgments, we have already seen in the discussion of inference in Chapter VIII of Part Two, other judgments grow.[1] It is, then, not enough to have judgments and to make immediate inferences from them; it is the nature of the human mind that it must verify its judgments, must affirm their truth, must follow the path they take and the direction they set; that it must discover and comprehend, synthesize and assent, examine and compare, and through what is known arrive at last at the unknown. In moving thus from one thing understood to another, from the known to the unknown, from one judgment to another and yet another, the mind is performing the third act which it of its nature is capable of. And this is reasoning.

Reasoning Defined

Reasoning may be defined simply as that act by which the mind, proceeding from a judgment, moves to a second judgment and thence, because of the inter-relationship of these two, to still a third judgment. It is the end toward which everything we have noted so far about apprehension and judgment leads. Mental life, we have noted repeatedly, begins with the concept; nevertheless thought or thinking, in the broader sense, as we have also observed, properly begins with the ordering of our concepts, or with judgment. But thinking, in the broadest sense of the word, is what we arrive at when we arrive at reasoning. Here, now, is the mind ordering its judgments, building upon them, moving with them from what it knows to what it is yet to know. Here is the mind doing what, in its nature, it is designed to do. Here is the mind in its wholeness. Here is mental life at its fullest.

In the station arcades and runways of the great metropolitan subway system of the city of New York you may read, stenciled in countless places on walls and posts, this sign, consisting of a single word: *Think*. Intended as a safety hint, this little sign, if one reflects a moment, becomes of admonitions the most momentous that man might visit upon himself — urging him as it does to do the one thing upon which, more than upon any other, the fullness of his human nature depends.

Kinds of Reasoning

There are two ways in which the mind discovers truth, arrives at the unknown, or reasons. These are called *deductive* and *inductive* reasoning.

Deductive reasoning is reasoning that literally (*de+duco*) leads out of something. It is reasoning from cause to effect, from universal judgments to particular ones. Example: All men are mortal; all Chinamen are men; therefore a Chinaman is mortal. Inductive reasoning is reasoning that literally (*in + duco*) leads into something. It is reasoning from effect to cause, from particular judgments to universal ones. Example: Washington was mortal, Jefferson was mortal, Lincoln was mortal; Washington, Jefferson, and Lincoln were men; therefore men are mortal.

Deduction, it is seen, then, is reasoning from the general to the particular; induction from the particular to the general. To put it in a figure: deduction is the descending in the elevator of thought from a universal law or principle to a particular application of the law or principle; induction is the ascending in the elevator of thought from the particular application to the universal law. In both cases the car opens at the same stop, which is *truth*. These are the two ways, then, in which the mind works. Both are equally natural to it. Between them there is no antipathy. They are not opposite things but complementary things.[2]

To the Student, an Elaboration

Perhaps you have noticed from what has been said so far about reasoning that, although in the progression of *acts of the mind* we move from the concept to the judgment and from the judgment to reasoning, when we arrive at reasoning and analyze it for what it is, we in effect return to the judgment. Reasoning moves from one judgment to a second, only to arrive at still another judgment. The judgment is thus seen to be the central act of all our intellectual life. That is why, we said earlier, a knowledge of the judgment and of its right uses is of incalculable importance. "He is a man of good judgment," if rightly meant, might be the most flattering of compliments. Good judgment is good reason. To judge rightly and well is *to reason* rightly and well.

CHAPTER X

The Internal Product of the Act: Mental Argumentation

Mental Argumentation Defined

We have already seen that the end product of the act of apprehension is the concept or mental word and the end product of the judgment is its mental statement. In like manner we speak of the end product of the act of reasoning, and we call it ratiocination or *mental argumentation.* It is a product because it is what the mind *forms* when it orders its judgments, that is to say when it searches for a manifestation or explanation of what is unknown or obscure or complex to it. Mental argumentation (*arguere,* to make clear) may thus be defined as the manifestation or representation of *the order* of the mind's judgments, of their inter-relationship or bearing or effect upon one another.

Components of Mental Argumentation

Mental argumentation has to do with a combination of logical forms, each of which is determined by the *constant* or *variable* character of the terms[3] of which the judgments at issue consist. Let us consider this combination of logical forms: *(If B is A) (and C is B) (then C is A).* We have, we see, three "logical forms", made up of three constants *(if) (and) (then)* and three "propositional variables" *(B is A) (C is B) (C is A).*[4]

Superimposed, as it were, on this relationship of parts is still a larger or more inclusive relationship. The mental argumentation *If B is A and C is B, then C is likewise A* may be seen, from the larger view, to consist of: First, the *antecedent*, the first two judgments or propositions (or what we shall learn shortly to call the "premises"). Second, the *consequent* (or what we shall learn to call the "conclusion"), consisting of the third judgment or proposition which grows out of the combination of the other two. Third, the *consequence*, growing out of the relation between the antecedent and consequent (*if, and, then,* etc.); that is to say, the *argument* itself.

Division of Mental Argumentation

A division of mental argumentation is possible according to the distinction made between the *matter* and the *form* of the argument.

Accordingly we speak of: 1) its *proximate matter*, the three propositional variables made up of or containing (always) only three variable terms (*B is A, C is B, C is A*), and 2) its *remote matter*, the three terms themselves (*A, B, C*). Thus, in the argument *If all whales are mammals and Moby Dick is a whale, then Moby Dick is a mammal* the proximate matter consists of the propositional variables (all whales are mammals) (Moby Dick is a whale) (Moby Dick is a mammal) and the remote matter consists of the three terms (whale) (mammal) (Moby Dick).

In accordance with the form of the argument, that is, the order or arrangement or disposition of the judgments, which may be good or bad in regard to the inference made, we further classify mental argumentation as 1) *valid* (if the antecedent really infers the consequent) or 2) *invalid* (if the antecedent does not infer the consequent). Example of a valid argument: If all men are bipeds and John is a man, then John is a biped. Example of an invalid argument: If all quadrupeds are animals and John is a man, then John is not a quadruped.

The Universal Law of Argumentation

Out of the nature of mental argumentation, its components and the relationship of its parts, arises what is called the universal law of argumentation, which may be explained in this way: In every valid argument, from a true antecedent a true consequent will always follow. From a false antecedent, however, a true consequent may follow by accident. That is to say, from the true always the true; from the false usually the false, but sometimes the true by accident.[5] Example of the last: (My purse is on the moon; the moon is in my pocket; therefore my purse is in my pocket.) In an invalid argument, on the other hand, the antecedent may be true while the consequent is false. Example: All men are mortal; dogs are not men; therefore dogs are not mortal. From the foregoing it is seen that the form of a mental argument assures us of its validity or consistency, and the matter assures us of its truth.

CHAPTER XI

The Sign of Argumentation: The Syllogism

The Syllogism Defined

Whereas the sign of the concept, as we have seen, is the term and the sign of the judgment is the proposition, the sign of argumentation is the *syllogism,* which may be defined simply as a group of two or more propositions so combined or disposed as to lead the mind to another proposition or other propositions. In accordance with the kinds of reasoning, previously described as deductive and inductive, there are two kinds of syllogisms: the *deductive syllogism* and the *inductive syllogism.*

The Deductive Syllogism

Defined:

We have already noted that the path or course or direction which the mind takes in moving from one judgment to another or to others is given the general name of *inference.* An inference is said to be immediate when it is one drawn directly from a single judgment or proposition (John is at home; therefore John is not away from home). An inference is said to be mediate when it is one drawn, not from a single proposition, but from two or more propositions *in combination* (John is a soldier; a soldier is not a sailor; therefore John is not a sailor). The form of this mediate inference, its outward expression, is what is called the *deductive syllogism.* It is defined formally, according to Aristotle,[6] as "an expression i.e. a manifestation of thought in which, certain things being stated, something other than what is stated follows of necessity from their being so." Less formally it may be defined as a group of three propositions, the third of which emerges as an inference out of the bearing the other two have upon each other.

Looked at analytically, the syllogism given above (John is a soldier; a soldier is not a sailor; therefore John is not a sailor), corresponding to the mental argumentation of which it is the sign, manifests a combination of logical forms. The first and second of these (John is soldier) (a soldier is not a sailor) we call the premises—a "premise" being, simply, a sentence or statement affirming or denying one thing of another.[7] The third of these (John is not a sailor) we call the *conclusion*. It will be noted here, as implied earlier, that the premises correspond to the antecedent of the mental argument and the conclusion to the consequent.

Looked at further, the syllogism manifests, also, a combination of terms, around which the premises and conclusion as logical forms are constructed; these are, in this case, *John, soldier, sailor.* Every syllogism consists of three such terms, two of which constitute what are called the *extremes* or the major and minor terms of the syllogism and the third the *middle term* of the syllogism. The middle term, it will be noted, is that one which appears *twice* in the *premises*.[8] Returning to our example: the extremes are *John* and *sailor;* the middle term is *soldier.*

Universal Principles:

From the nature of the deductive syllogism derive several "universal principles" governing its right use. These are three. The first, called the principle of triple identity and separating third, is that two terms both of which are identical with a common third term are identical with each other, and that two terms one of which is identical with a common third term and the other not identical with the common third term are not identical with each other. (Examples: If B is A and C is B, then C is A. If B is A and C is not B, then C is not A.) The second, called the principle of *all* (*de omni*) and *none* (*de nullo*),[9] is that that which is universally affirmed of a term is affirmed of everything contained within that term, and that which is universally denied of a term is denied of everything contained within that term. (Examples: Koreans are yellow-skinned people; Syngman Rhee is a yellow-skinned person. The human body is not immortal; the human heart is not immortal.) The third, called the principle of the universality of the middle term, is that the middle term must be understood at least once in the antecedent as a universal concept, or as an objective note of a universal essence. (Example: Koreans are yellow-skinned people; Syngman Rhee is a *Korean;* therefore Syngman Rhee is a yellow-skinned person.)[10]

Categorical or Assertoric Syllogism:

A categorical or assertoric syllogism is one in which the premises are *categorical propositions.* A categorical proposition, it will be remembered, is one in which the copula expresses an absolute relationship (*is, is not*) between the subject and the predicate. Certain rules, or restrictions, arising out of the nature of the categorical syllogism, govern its use. The so-called "rules of the categorical syllogism" are eight in number:

(1) There must be only three terms.

(2) The terms must never be more inclusive in the conclusion than they are in the premises.

(3) The middle term must never be found in the conclusion.

LOGIC OF ARGUMENTATION 87

(4) The middle term must be understood in at least one of the premises as a universal.
(5) From two negative premises no conclusion is possible.
(6) From two affirmative premises a negative conclusion is not possible.
(7) From two particular premises no conclusion is possible.
(8) The conclusion always follows the inferior premise (premises being inferior or superior to one another on the basis of quantity and quality; e.g., a particular is inferior to a universal, a negative is inferior to an affirmative).[11]

Figures and Moods of Categorical Syllogisms:

By the *figure* of a syllogism is meant the disposition or arrangement of the terms within the premises.[12] The four figures that a categorical syllogism may assume are distinguished by the position of the middle term.[13] These four figures may be seen graphically, as follows:

	1	2	3	4
(Proposition 1):	B-A	A-B	B-A	A-B
(Proposition 2):	C-B	C-B	B-C	B-C
(Proposition 3):	C-A	C-A	C-A	C-A

Remembering, now, that the middle term (B) is that one which appears twice in the premises, in all four figures, the other two terms (A and C) are referred to as the extremes of the syllogism in the light of their relation to the middle term. It is to be noted that, in the case of the first figure, A contains B and B contains C.[14] In the second figure, B contains A and A contains C.[15] In the third figure, A contains C and C contains B.[16] This may be shown graphically, as follows:

Figure 1: B-A
          C-B $A > B > C$
          ―――
          C-A

Figure 2:   A-B
              C-B   B > A > C
              ―――
              C-A

Figure 3:   B-A
              B-C   A > C > B
              ―――
              C-A

In the fourth figure, *A* is contained in *B* and *B* is contained in *C*:[17]

Figure 4:   A-B
              B-C   A < B < C
              ―――   (or C > B > A, which is the reverse
              C-A   of figure one)

By the *mood* of a syllogism is meant the disposition and the kinds of the propositions used in the premises. Recalling, now, the four classifications of propositions, *A, E, I, O,* and considering for a moment that, theoretically, we might have such an assortment of dispositions and kinds as

Proposition 1 (major): A A A A, E E E E,
Proposition 2 (minor): A E I O, A E I O,   etc.

we would seem to have (keeping in mind that there are four figures and that proposition 1 may be substituted for proposition 2 and vice versa) sixty-four possible moods — 4 x 4 x 4 = 64. A moment's analysis of these possibilities, in the light of the rules governing the syllogism, however, will show that of the sixty-four only eight of these moods are valid ones. The eight valid moods of the syllogism may be represented graphically, as follows:

Proposition 1 (major): A A A A E E I O
Proposition 2 (minor): A E I O A I A A   etc.

In the case of all moods, the disposition of the premises is not to be considered as fixed; that is to say, the major and the minor, or propositions 1 and 2, may be interchanged in position. This is so because in any given syllogism the major premise need not be, and indeed frequently is not, stated first.[18] The conclusion of any syllogism is the consequent of the antecedent; the same antecedent, regardless of the disposition of its parts (the premises), will always result in the same conclusion. The conclusion, or proposition 3, it is to be noted also, is itself a proposition[19]— and as such partakes of the properties of propositions, i.e. it is subject to conversion, obversion, opposition, and is productive of other judgments or immediate inferences.

Integration of Moods and Figures:

When the same syllogism (i.e. *the same terms*) is put through all four figures, with the appropriate changes in the mood of the premises, and respecting the "rules of the categorical syllogism," it is readily seen that the conclusion is not always the same; that is to say, one figure will produce one conclusion and another another.[20]

In the case of the first figure, the conclusions possible are A, E, I, O.[21] The moods resulting in these conclusions are four:

A	E	A	E
A	A	I	I
A	E	I	O

In the case of the second figure, the conclusions are all negative ones, E and O, whether universal or particular.[22] The moods of the second figure are again four:

E	A	E	A
A	E	I	O
E	E	O	O

In the case of the third figure, a universal conclusion, either affirmative or negative, is impossible.[23] The conclusions are, therefore, either *I* or *O*. The moods of the third figure are six:

A	I	A	E	O	E
A	A	I	A	A	I
—	—	—	—	—	—
I	I	I	O	O	O

In the case of the fourth figure, the conclusions possible are *E, I, O*. No *A*, or universal affirmative, conclusion is possible.²⁴ The moods of this fourth, or indirect first, figure are five:

A	E	I	E	E
A	A	A	A	I
—	—	—	—	—
I	E	I	O	O

Perfect Figure, Perfect Moods, and Perfect Syllogism:

Of all four figures the first is readily seen to be the most nearly perfect, for two reasons. First: it is the only figure in which all conclusions, *A, E, I, O,* are possible. Second: the conclusions are all deduced or proved by means of the premises originally taken;²⁵ that is, they need nothing other than what has been stated to make plain what necessarily follows.²⁶

The perfect moods, of the first figure, are:

A	E
A	A
—	—
A	E

because their conclusions are universal and because the third and fourth moods can be reduced to these first two.²⁷ The first figure, in either of the two perfect moods, constitutes the perfect syllogism.

Reduction of Syllogisms (Imperfect to Perfect):

An imperfect syllogism may be reduced to a perfect one by either of two methods: 1) *by converting it* and 2) *by reducing it to the impossible.*²⁸

LOGIC OF ARGUMENTATION

Imperfect syllogisms of the second, third, and fourth figures may be reduced to the first figure and its moods by conversion. Example:

Mood: E   Figure: No *A* is *B*
           I   Some *C* is *B*
           ―   ―――――――――
           O   Some *C* is not *A*

By converting the negative premise (proposition 1) simply, the figure, which here is the second, is reduced to the first, with the conclusion still the same:

No *B* is *A*
Some *C* is *B*
―――――――――
Some *C* is not *A*

Not all moods can be reduced to the first figure by conversion. Consider these moods:

A   O
O   A
―   ―
O   O

In the first case, the conversion of proposition 1 would result in an *I* proposition; we know that from *I* and *O* no conclusion is possible. In the second case, it will be recalled that an *O* proposition cannot be converted.[29]

When a syllogism cannot be reduced to the first figure by conversion it may be done so by reducing it to the impossible (*reductio ad impossibile*). Consider the following cases:

Figure 2:	All *A* is *B*	(A)
	Some *C* is not *B*	(O)
	Some *C* is not *A*	(O)
Figure 3:	Some *B* is not *A*	(O)
	All *B* is *C*	(A)
	Some *C* is not *A*	(O)

Reducing these two moods to the perfect mood (A) (A)/(A) cannot be done directly, but must be done, instead, indirectly, as follows:
1) We accept the premises (A) (O) and (O) (A) as true;
2) We take the contradictory of the conclusion, in both cases an (O), and affirm it as (A): (All C is A);
3) We substitute this (A) for one of the premises, in both cases the (O);
4) We arrive at a perfect syllogism (A) (A)/(A), in which the conclusion (A) is the contradictory of an (O) accepted as true. We are forced, however, to reject such an (A) conclusion; not rejecting it would result in an absurdity or impossibility, since we cannot deny both (A) and (O) at the same time.

In the cases of the moods in figures 2 and 3 given above, then, it is seen that the validity of the conclusions (and hence of the syllogisms) is upheld and the moods themselves are seen to be valid ones, since they have been submitted to the test of a perfect mood, (A) (A)/(A), not directly (i.e., not by being reduced to it) but indirectly (i.e., by means of it).

Modal Syllogisms:

A modal syllogism is one in which one of the premises is a modal proposition.[30] A modal proposition, again, is one in which the copula expresses a relationship between subject and predicate of *possibility* (can), *impossibility* (cannot), *contingency* (may), or *necessity* (must). An important rule governs the modal syllogism; it may be expressed thusly: the modality of the modal proposition (premise) must be maintained in the conclusion of the syllogism. Example: All B may be A; all C is B; therefore all C may be A.

The Enthymeme:

A syllogism incompletely expressed because of the omission of one of its parts (proposition 1, 2) is called an *enthymeme*.

In the case of an enthymeme, we must find for ourselves the missing part.[31] This is done in the following ways:
   a) If proposition 1 is missing:
      Proposition 2 will give us the middle term
      The conclusion will give us the two other terms
   b) If proposition 2 is missing:
      Proposition 1 will give us the middle term
      The conclusion will give us the two other terms

Sorites:

Sorites is the name given to a group or aggregation of related syllogisms made up of connected propositions in which the predicate of the first is the subject of the second, the predicate of the second, the subject of the third, and so on. It is, in short, an elongated syllogism in which there is a multiplicity of middle terms. Example:

$$\begin{array}{c} \text{If all } B \text{ is } A \\ \text{and all } A \text{ is } C \\ \text{and all } C \text{ is } D \\ \text{and all } D \text{ is } F \\ \hline \text{then all } B \text{ is } F \end{array}$$

It will be noted that, even though several middle terms are necessary to establish the relation between B and F, the figure is the same as if only one middle term were involved.[32]

Compound Syllogisms:

The sorites is not to be confused with the compound syllogism, which is a syllogism in which at least one of the premises is a compound or complex proposition. A compound or complex proposition, it will be recalled, is one containing a multiplicity of subjects or copulas or predicates — a multiplicity indicated explicitly or implicitly according to the grammar of the proposition itself. It is obvious that when a premise is complex, the complexity it brings to the syllogism must be recognized and dealt with properly.

Kinds of Compound Syllogisms:

There are as many kinds of compound syllogisms as there are kinds of compound propositions. Among these are:

(a) *Conjunctive* or *disjunctive syllogism:* a syllogism in which one of the premises is a proposition containing a conjunctive or disjunctive connective (*and, or, either, neither, nor, but*). Examples:

| A cannot be both B and C | B is either A or C |
A is B	B is A
A cannot be C	B is not C

It will be noted that these syllogisms lead nowhere until the certitude of proposition 1 (in both cases) is determined either *constructively* (by accepting one of the possibilities) or *destructively* (by rejecting one of the possibilities) in proposition 2.

b) *Conditional syllogism:* a syllogism in which one of the premises is a conditional proposition, i.e. a proposition containing a conditional connective (*if*). Let us note, here, that a conditional proposition (if A is B, A is C) consists really of two parts: a) the *condition* (If A is B) and b) the *conditioned* (A is C). From this fact derive the following rules for the conditional syllogism:[33]

1) To affirm the condition is to accept the conditioned,
2) To affirm the conditioned is not to accept the condition,
3) To reject the condition is not to reject the conditioned,
4) To reject the conditioned is to reject the condition.

c) *Causal syllogism:* a syllogism in which one of the premises is a causal proposition, i.e. a proposition containing the connective *because*. Obviously a causal syllogism can readily be converted to a conditional one (*because* being the logical equivalent of *if*); the rules governing the conditional syllogism, therefore, apply as well to the causal syllogism.

d) *The dilemma:* a disjunctive syllogism so constructed that, no matter which part of the disjunctive premise is affirmed, the same conclusion follows. In this, the disjunction must be complete; if not, we fall into what is called "the paradox" or "sophism". Example:

>Logicians are either right or wrong.
>If they are right, they do not need logic.
>If they are wrong, logic is of no help to them.
>In either case logic is useless.

Polysyllogism:

The *polysyllogism,* not to be confused with the sorites, is a series of syllogisms so related that the conclusion of one is the premise of another, and so on. Example:

>1) Every B is A
>   Every C is B
>2) Every C is A
>   Every D is C
>3) Every D is A
>   Every E is D
>   Every E is A

Classification of Deductive Syllogisms:

Apart from the distinctions made above, deductive syllogisms may be classified, according to the *matter* of the premises, into four classes: *demonstrative, probable, erroneous,* and *fallacious.*[34]

A demonstrative syllogism is one whose premises are concerned with necessary matter, that is to say, primary or basic truths (All men must die). A premise is a necessary one if its predicate is an element in the essential nature of the subject or if the subject is part of the essential nature of the predicate.[35] The predicate likewise must be *universal,* in the sense that it applies equally to all subjects of which it is affirmed or denied;[36] it must be *primary,* in the sense that it must be attributed to the subject as a first thing to be attributed to the subject.[37] The conclusion of a demonstrative syllogism is an object of certainty.

A probable syllogism is one whose premises are concerned with probable matter, that is to say, a syllogism which proceeds from opinions accepted by most people, by the majority of scholars, scientists, those especially fitted to make judgments about the matter at issue. In this case the conclusion is an object of opinion.

An erroneous syllogism is one whose premises are contentious and whose conclusion does not follow from the premises in accordance with the rules of deductive reasoning. The conclusion is thus an object of error. An erroneous syllogism which is a deliberate attempt to mislead or deceive is called, more specifically, a fallacious one.

Fallacies in Deductive Reasoning:

Fallacious deductive reasoning may be of two kinds: 1) a violation of the rules of syllogistic reasoning or 2) a falling into the common pitfalls of everyday thinking. Among these common pitfalls or everyday fallacies are the following:

1) *Equivocation:* the use of equivocal, and hence undefined, terms. This becomes, as well, a fallacy by way of a violation of the rule that a deductive syllogism contains not more than 3 terms. (Example: California is a state; a state is a condition; therefore California is a condition.)

2) *Accident:* the confusion of accidental with essential attributes, the assumption that the subject and predicate of a premise are identical and hence what is true of the subject (even though accidental) is true of the predicate and vice versa. (Example: Wine is an inebriating beverage; John has had some wine; therefore John is inebriated.)

3) *Absolute and Qualified Statements:* the confusion of what is generally true with what is specifically true and vice versa, or the confusion of universals with particulars and vice versa. (Example: Chinese are yellow-skinned people; Syngman Rhee is a yellow-skinned person; therefore Syngman Rhee is a Chinese.)
4) *Ignoring the Issue:* the avoiding of, evading, or skirting the conclusion, the talking for talk's sake, the failure to get to the point, etc. (Example: Chinese are yellow-skinned people; Syngman Rhee is a yellow-skinned person; Syngman Rhee almost ruined the chances for a truce; he is an old man and doesn't see the long-range issues, etc.)
5) *Begging the Question:* assuming as true what is to be proved before it is proved, reasoning in a circle or redundantly, proving one thing to be a second by means of a third whose truth depends on the first. (Example: Mary cannot go to school because she is ill; that she is ill must explain why she is not at school; therefore she cannot go to school because she is ill.

The Inductive Syllogism

Defined:

It will be remembered, again, that the deduction syllogism shows a movement of the mind from premises (the antecedent) to a conclusion (the consequent), or from the general principle to the particular application of it. Induction, we have noted, is the reverse of deduction. It is a movement of the mind from the particular application of a principle to the principle itself. Whereas the form of deductive reasoning is the deductive syllogism, again, that of inductive reasoning is the inductive syllogism.[38] An inductive syllogism is a group of three propositions in the reverse order in which they would be found in a deductive syllogism. Example:

Proposition 1: Plants, brutes, and men move themselves

Proposition 2: Plants, brutes, and men are all living organisms

Proposition 3: All living organisms move themselves

Figuratively:

$$\frac{\begin{array}{l} B < A \\ B = C \end{array}}{C < A}$$

When one reflects that, as has been shown, deduction proceeds from an antecedent to a consequent, from premises affirmed to a conclusion inferred, one might ask whence the antecedent? Where do we get our premises? Where do we get the primary premise which, as we have seen, is necessary to every demonstrative syllogism. The answer is that we get it by means of induction.[39] Man is a sensory creature: he sees, he listens, he smells, he touches, he feels, he weighs, he measures. He observes, examines whatever he encounters, whatever is around him. Sense perception has to do with the particular, but the objects of sense perception have to do with the universal. Man sees not the essence of things, their genus, or even their species; what he sees and touches are particular things from which inductively he infers their essence, their genus, their species.[40]

Universal Principle:

From the nature of the inductive syllogism derives the law of *all (de omni)* or *none (de nullo)*: whatever is affirmed or denied of all the particulars is also affirmed or denied of the universal.

Insufficient and Sufficient Induction:

Induction may be *insufficient,* as when so few particulars are known that no universal conclusion is warranted, or *sufficient,* as when enough particulars are known that a universal conclusion is not only warranted but reasonably inferred. The latter type constitutes the method of the physical or experimental sciences and in this connection is referred to as the *scientific method,* to be dealt with in greater detail in the next chapter.

SUPPLEMENTARY READINGS FOR CHAPTER XI

Abraham, L., "A Note on the Fruitfulness of Deduction," *Philosophy of Science,* vol. 3, 1936, pp. 152-155.
Aristotle, *Analytica Priora,* 24a 10 - 70b 38.
————, *Analytica Posteriora,* 71a 1-100b 17.
Bahm, A. J., "New Rules for Sorites," *The New Scholasticism,* vol. 20, 1946, pp. 323-333.
Bennett, O., "St. Thomas' Theory of Demonstrative Proof," *Proceedings of the American Catholic Philosophical Association,* vol. 15, 1941, pp. 76-88.
Black, M., "A New Method of Presentation of the Theory of the Syllogism," *Journal of Philosophy,* vol. 42, (August, 1945), pp. 449-455.
Bochenski, I. M., "On the Categorical Syllogism," *Dominican Studies,* vol. 1, 1948, pp. 1-23.
Churchman, C. W., "Statistics, Pragmatics, Induction," *Philosophy of Science,* vol. 15, 1948, pp. 249-268.
Creed, I. P., "The Justification of the Habit of Induction," *Journal of Philosophy,* vol. 37, (February, 1940), pp. 85-97.
Dubs, H. H., "Deduction," *Rational Induction,* The University of Chicago Press, Chicago, Illinois, 1930, pp. 142-215.
Edwards, P., "Russell's Doubts about Induction," *Mind,* vol. 58, (April, 1949), pp. 141-163.
Greenwood, T., "The Characters of the Aristotelian Logic," *The Thomist,* vol. 4, 1942, pp. 221-246.
Henle, P., "On the Fourth Figure of the Syllogism," *Philosophy of Science,* vol. 16, 1949, pp. 94-104.
Johnstone. H W. Jr., "Philosophy and Argumentum ad Hominem," *Journal of Philosophy,* vol. 49, (July, 1952), pp. 489-498.
Kapp, E., *Greek Foundations of Traditional Logic,* Columbia University Press, New York, 1942, pp. 60-74.
Klubertanz, G. P., "Logic or Experience," *The Modern Schoolman,* vol. 15, 1938, pp. 36-38.

Lukasiewicz, J., *Aristotle's Syllogistic,* Clarendon Press, Oxford, 1951.
Mabbott, J. D., "Two Notes on Syllogism," *Mind,* vol. 48, (July, 1939), pp. 326-337.
Moody, E. A., *The Logic of William of Ockham,* Sheed and Ward, New York, 1935, pp. 220-312.
Parry, W. T., "On Numerical Moods of the Syllogism," *Philosophy and Phenomenological Research,* vol. 9, (March, 1950), pp. 408-413.
Plockmann, G. K., "Professor Henle on the Four Figures of Syllogism," *Philosophy of Science,* vol. 19, 1952, pp. 333-341.
Popkin, R. H., "An Examination of Two Inconsistencies in Aristotelian Logic," *The Philosophical Review,* vol. 56, 1947, pp. 670-681.
Quine, W. V., "On Natural Deduction," *The Journal of Symbolic Logic,* vol. 15, 1950, pp. 93-102.
Reade, W. H. V., *The Problem of Inference,* Clarendon Press, Oxford, 1938, pp. 3-46.
Reichenbach, H., "The Syllogism Revised," *Philosophy of Science,* vol. 19, 1952, pp. 1-16.
Ross, W. D., "The Discovery of The Syllogism," *The Philosophical Review,* vol. 48, 1939, pp. 251-272.
Shur, E., "The Theory of the Concept, the Judgment, and the Inference in Formal and Dialectic Logic," *Philosophy and Phenomenological Research,* vol. 5, (December, 1944), pp. 199-216.
Simon, Y. R. and Menger, K., "Aristotelian Demonstration and Postulational Method," *The Modern Schoolman,* vol. 25, 1948, pp. 183-192.
Solmsen, F., "Aristotle's Syllogism and Its Platonic Background," *The Philosophical Review,* vol. 60, 1951, pp. 563-571.
————, "The Discovery of the Syllogism," *The Philosophical Review,* vol. 50, 1941, pp. 410-421.
Stakelum, J. W., "Why 'Galenian Figure'?" *The New Scholasticism,* vol. 16, 1942, pp. 289-296.
Toohey, J. J., "Schiller's Attack on Formal Logic," *The Modern Schoolman,* vol. 16, 1938, pp. 17-20.
Veatch, H., "In Defense of the Syllogism," *The Modern Schoolman,* vol. 27, 1950, pp. 184-202.

Veatch, H., *Intentional Logic,* Yale University Press, New Haven, 1952, pp. 286-316.
————, "The Significance of Current Criticisms of the Syllogism," *The Thomist,* vol. 15, 1952, pp. 624-641.
Will, F. L., "Is There a Problem of Induction?" *Journal of Philosophy,* vol. 39, (September, 1942), pp. 505-513.
Wilson, J. C., *Statement and Inference,* Clarendon Press, Oxford, 1926, vol. II, pp. 412-552.

FOOTNOTES TO PART THREE

1. *Topica,* 112a 17: "Anyone who has made any statement whatever has in a certain sense made several statements, inasmuch as each statement has a number of necessary consequences; e.g. the man who has said 'X is a man' has also said that X is an animal, that X is animate, etc."
2. *An. Post.,* 81a 39.
3. Chap. III, p. 31; Chap. VII, p. 55 above.
4. *An. Post.,* 98b 5-10; *An. Pr.,* 34a 22 ff.
    I. M. Bocheński, O.P., *La Logique de Théophaste,* Librairie de l'Université de Fribourg, Suisse, 1947, p. 115: "The propositional variables appear for the first time in Aristotle."
5. *An. Pr.,* 53b 4.
6. *An. Pr.* 24b 18; *Topica,* 100a 25.
7. *An. Pr.,* 24a 16.
8. *An. Pr.,* 47a 38.
9. *An. Pr.,* 25b 32; 53b 9; 57a 40 - b17.
10. *S.T.,* I a, q. 13, a. 12. See: the nature of a true affirmative proposition, Chap. VII, p. 56 above.
11. *An. Pr.,* 25b 8, 40b 30, 41b 6-7, 41b 36, 42a 32, 44b 40, 47b 26, 47b 40 - 48a 28.
12. *An. Pr.,* 47a 37 - 40.
13. *An. Pr.,* 47b 13.
14. *An. Pr.,* 25b 35.
15. *An. Pr.,* 26b 36.
16. *An. Pr.,* 28a 12.
17. It has now been established that the fourth figure and its moods were known and accepted by Aristotle, therefore not discovered by Galen. The reason given for the omission of

this figure by Aristotle in his systematic exposé of the syllogistic theory (*Analytica Priora*, Book I, Chaps. 4-6) is that Book I, Chap. 7 and Book II, Chap. 1 were composed at a later date than Book I, Chaps. 4-6. See I. M. Bocheński, O.P., *La Logique de Théophraste*, p. 59.

18. The order of the premises is arbitrary since the antecedent (being complex or multiple) brings about the conclusion. The premises of the antecedent are commutable or transposable. See J. Lukasiewicz, *Aristotle's Syllogistic*, Oxford, Clarendon Press, 1951, p. 33-34. For examples of syllogisms with transposed premises see: 28a 26, 28b 7, 28b 12, 28b 26, 60a 3, 60a 5, 61b 41. Aristotle transposed even the AA/A mood; see 61b 34.
19. *An. Pr.*, 53 a 8.
20. *An. Pr.*, 50a 5-10.
21. *An. Pr.*, 26b 30.
22. *An. Pr.*, 28a 7.
23. *An. Pr.*, 29a 17.
24. *An. Pr.*, 28b 7, 29a 19, 53a 4.
25. *An. Pr.*, 26b 30.
26. *An. Pr.*, 24b 22.
27. *An. Pr.*, 29b, 1.
28. *An. Pr.*, 27a 6, 28a 19, 29a 30; 27a 38, 59b 28.
29. See above, Chap. VII, p. 66.
30. *An. Pr.*, 29b 36; see above, Chap. VII, p. 57; 40b 16, 28-35.
31. *An. Pr.*, 47a 13.
32 *An. Pr.*, 41a 18.
33. It would be well to note the distinction made by Thomas Aquinas (Ia, q. 14, a. 13, ad 2um) between an antecedent which is the remote necessary cause and a consequent which is a contingent effect; such as: *If the sun moves, the grass will grow.*
34. *Topica*, 100a 25 ff., *An. Pr.*, 46a 9, *An. Post.*, 81b 17.
35. *An. Post.*, 73a 34-40.
36. *An. Post.*, 73a 27.
37. *An. Post.*, 73a 33 - 74a 3.
38. *An. Post.*, 81b 41, *An. Pr.*, 68b 15, 68b 36.
39. *An. Post.*, 100b 4.
40. *An. Post.*, 100a 15. . . . "for though the act of sense-perception is of the particular, its content is universal. . . ."

Part Four

CONTEMPORARY PROBLEMS

Scientific Method
The Old and the New
Logical Positivism
Propaganda

CHAPTER XII

The Scientific Method

The Role of Induction in Human Reason

The human mind, as we have seen, reasons from the general to the particular and from the particular to the general. Deduction and induction are thus the two paths along which the mind moves when it reasons. Every man every waking day of his life lives by both these mental processes; without them he could not get along in even the most mundane of daily activities. Of the two, deduction might be regarded as the more *refined* mental process; moving from judgments affirmed, it builds, as it were, a conclusion, by *thought* or *reason* in the purest sense. Induction, however, is the more ubiquitous. The deductive syllogism itself implies induction, because (although all intellectual knowledge comes ultimately through first principles which are the result of experience) we may say that it is by means of induction that we arrive at our premises or antecedent out of which derives our consequent. The mind, that is to say, seeks for, searches out, uncovers enough particulars to make a universal affirmation (e.g. a premise) reasonable. This seeking for, this searching out, this uncovering of particulars is what is meant by scientific inquiry or investigation. It is man's means for lifting himself out of the chaos of his ignorance, for arriving at premises, for reaching certitude in knowledge, for solving the problems of his natural existence.

Some Preliminaries to a Definition of Scientific Method

The scientific method presupposes a scientific mind. What precisely is meant by a *scientific mind?* From the more general standpoint, the characteristics of the scientific mind may be said to be three: It is, first of all, *objective;* it is impartial, unprejudiced; it is not predisposed; it does not find before it has begun to seek. The scientific mind is *exacting;* it is not slipshod, haphazard, imprecise; it wants data and it wants all the data possible of attainment. The scientific mind is *critical;* it is not precipitant; it is judicious, circumspect; it does not grasp but stops and considers, measures and weighs. From the more particular standpoint, the qualities of character of the possessor of a scientific mind may likewise be said to be three: He is, first of all, *submissive* in the face of facts, deferential to the truth even when the truth is not to his liking. He is by nature *mathematical,* that is to say, given to symbols, abbreviated representations, imaginative configurations; mathematics he reduces to equations, chemistry he reduces to formulae, classification of data he reduces to statistics. He is, in his outlook, *resolute;* he is a seeker of, not a toy-er with, truth.

The student would do well here to consider how large a part is played by the principles and processes of logic, by the laws of thought (in other words), in bringing about this "scientific attitude."

The Scientific Method Defined

The scientific method, now, may be defined as the systematic application of the principles and processes of logic to scientific inquiry in general and to the special objects of the various sciences in particular. More specifically it might be regarded as: a term to designate the structure of the various sciences. The latter has meaning as a definition when one considers that the structure of any science is determined essentially by:

a) the proper object of the science;

b) the manner of its development;

c) the kind of generalizations it involves;

d) its philosophical foundations;

e) its relationship with and application to other sciences.[1]

The scientific method is not understood here to be the method of "naturalism", "logical empiricism", or "logical positivism". For a treatment of this other the student is referred to Chapter XIV below.

All sciences are, before anything else, a search for causes, reasons, and determining conditions. Since the dawn of civilization, it has been the universal experience of mankind that things do not happen without reason, that a given phenomenon must have a given cause, that (given the same conditions) the same causes will produce the same effects, that there is, in short, order and law in nature. We speak of the natural *order* and not without reason. Upon this principle of causality science, itself, builds. And the logical foundation of the scientific method lies precisely in the fact that the various sciences correspond simply to the various formulations of this principle.

The searching for, the seeking out, the uncovering of causes, reasons, and determining conditions, which is the problem of science and the scientific method is a problem properly described as epistemological. That is to say, it is the problem of knowledge, of the value of knowledge, of its limits and capacities. It consists essentially of the abstraction from the sensible by the intellect of the singular to reach the universal, proceeding always on the principle that a characteristic constantly discernible in the individual or singular manifestations of a thing must belong to the essence of the thing. Thus, the problem of the scientific method or of scientific induction is precisely the problem of *knowledge itself*.

The Three-Fold Manner of Inductive Inference

Man as a sensory creature, knowing the world about him by a process of inductive inference, proceeds in fact in a threefold manner. First, he *observes;* that is to say, passively he "takes in" (with varying degrees of deliberateness) what his senses perceive. Second, he *experiments;* that is to say, actively he goes about setting up the conditions for special and particular sense perceptions, usually with some preconceived end, an "hypothesis", in his mind. Third, he *makes analogies;* that is to say, he attempts as far as possible to compare what he already knows with what he is trying to know; he attempts as far as possible to extend or build upon any relationship of resemblance between what is known and what is getting to be known.

Observation

Observation, which might be defined simply as *mental attention*, is to be distinguished from sensation, in so far as it involves a willed recognition of experience, the focusing of consciousness on facts, occurences, things. It is man looking at, noting, being aware. It is what every normal, rational human being does almost every waking moment of his day. When he does not, we have a name for him, and call him stargazer, dreamer, "mope."

The limitations of observation as a method of induction are fairly obvious. As a method it is limited by time and space and the bounds of human capacity and capability. To observe whether or not Haley's comet will make its next ten visits to our solar system on schedule would, indeed, require of the observer a life-time considerably longer than that now ordained for mortals. To observe the effects of a light filter on a kodachrome transparency would require an observer who was at least not color blind. Some natural facts, of course, cannot be observed (the transmutation of bread into bone). Others cannot be observed except at great cost, if not only in money then in life and limb. The dubious effects of new vaccines are not observed in mice, rats, and guinea pigs for reasons only of economy. The bent rod in the water which is not bent at all is, further, an example of fallacious observation. The subjectivity, the possibility of error, the natural limitations of observation as a method of induction make it less extensive, less effective than the method of experimentation.

Experimentation

Defined:

Experimentation, as suggested above, consists of the procedures utilized to verify "hypotheses" or preconceived generalizations or, in fact, the premises from which deduction proceeds. As a method of induction it might formally be defined as the alteration of phenomena, or of the method of and conditions for observing phenomena, in order to obtain knowledge about them. As distinguished from the procedures of deduction, which are described as *a priori* or *ante factum* (i.e. reasoning before the fact), the procedures of experimentation, being inductive, are described as *a posteriori* or *post factum* (i.e. reasoning after the fact) — accepting as their essential criterion the constancy of the phenomenal relations, based on the principle of causality.

Experimental Techniques:

In the altering of the methods of and conditions for observing phenomena in order to obtain knowledge about them, the experimenter recognizes readily the possibility and practicality of "rules of procedure" or experimental techniques. The job of the experimenter is, in fact, to reduce and isolate the conditions under which a given effect is found to be conjoined with a given cause, in the hope of proving or verifying by inference the cause-effect relationship. Toward this end, he makes use of procedures or techniques or, indeed, "methods."

Among the first to recognize the rôle of techniques in inductive inference was Sir Francis Bacon, who, on the basis of the criterion of *constant coincidence* (the same cause always produces the same effect) founded the so-called *Baconian Tables*. These are three in number:

1) The table of presence (*posita causa, ponitur effectus*): a cause being posited, its effect is posited.

2) The table of absence (*sublata causa, tollitur effectus*): a cause being absent, its effect is absent.

3) The table of degrees (*variante causa, variatur effectus*): a cause being variable, its effect is variable.

The relationship of these tables to the scientific method is, of course, obvious; and all that needs to be noted here about them is that, though they are needful and practical, they are incomplete, in the sense that whereas they can help to suggest an "hypothesis" they cannot prove it.

Coming after Bacon, John Stuart Mill, in working out "rules of general procedure," formulated his well-known *canons* or regulating principles based on what he called the "methods of experimental inquiry." These are five in number:[2]

1) *The Method of Agreement*:

If two or more instances of the phenomenon under investigation have only one circumstance in common, the circum-

stance in which alone all the instances agree is the cause (or effect) of the given phenomenon.

(Example):   ABC = a
               AMN = a
               ─────────
Therefore: A = a

2) *The Method of Difference:*

If an instance in which the phenomenon under investigation occurs, and an instance in which it does not occur, have every circumstance in common save one, that one occurring only in the former; the circumstance in which alone the two instances differ is the effect, or the cause, or an indispensable part of the cause, of the phenomenon.

(Example):   ABC = a
               BC = o
               ─────────
Therefore: A = a

3) *The Joint Method of Agreement and Difference:*

If two or more instances in which the phenomenon occurs have only one circumstance in common, while two or more instances in which it does not occur have nothing in common save the absence of that circumstance, the circumstance in which alone the two sets of instances differ is the effect, or the cause, or an indispensable part of the cause, of the phenomenon.

(Example):   ABC = a   DBC = d
               AMN = a   BC = o
               ─────────
Therefore: A = a

4) *The Method of Residues:*

Subduct from any phenomenon such part as is known by previous inductions to be the effect of certain antecedents, and the residue of the phenomenon is the effect of the remaining antecedents.

(Example):
$$\begin{aligned} ABCX &= abcx \\ A &= a \\ B &= b \\ C &= c \end{aligned}$$

Therefore: $X = x$

5) *The Method of Concomitant Variations:*

Whatever phenomenon varies in any manner whenever another phenomenon varies in some particular manner, is either a cause or an effect of that phenomenon, or is connected with it through some fact of causation.

(Example):
$$\begin{aligned} ABC &= a \\ 14A, 28B, C &= 14a \end{aligned}$$

Therefore: $A = a$

Concerning these methods and canons, the following things ought to be noted. The weakness of the first (agreement) is that it fails to take into account *fortuitous* agreement, that is, agreement by accident rather than necessity. The second (difference) is obviously more informative and more reliable than the first. The third (joint), of course, has the disadvantage of the first and the advantages of the second. The fourth (residue) is properly a method of circumscribing or giving shape to the investigation; its function is not so much to determine causes as to point the direction which the investigation ought not to take. The fifth (concomitant variations) has the advantage that it can be used in many cases in which the method of difference cannot be used.

Analogy

By analogy is meant a process of inductive inference based upon the awareness of a relationship of likeness or resemblance or comparison between one phenomenon and another or between one circumstance and another. Mill, again, expounded the principle of inference by analogy in this way: "Two things resemble each other in one or more respects; a certain proposition is true of one, therefore it is true of the other."[3]

Like observation, analogy as a manner of inductive inference is less extensive and less effective than experimentation. Not a little of what man knows he gets to know by analogy. He knows what an igloo is by comparing it to what he knows his house is and his house is not. But the limitations and disadvantages of analogy are as much a source of error and fallacy as the efficacy of it is a source of probability. Not infrequently the analogy leads to the hasty generalization. Because two things are alike in some respects, it is assumed they are alike in all respects; when, in fact, experimentation may show that they are not. What is important to remember is that in a valid analogy only essential resemblances have value. And the significance of essential differences, also, must not be overlooked. The efficacy of any analogy depends upon the ratio of significant resemblances to insignificant differences. If there were in the world two things that were perfectly alike in all respects, we might have an absolute analogy. We know, however, that this is not the case. The most that we can hope for from analogy, then, is probability not certainty. Jones has received an "A" in history; Smith has received an "A" in history. Jones has received a "B" in calculus; Smith has received a "B" in calculus. It may be inferred that Smith and Jones *probably* have the same I.Q. Light, like sound, moves outward from a common center; like sound, it can be reflected; when it is, as in the case of sound, the angle of reflection can be related to the angle of incidence. From this, it might be inferred that light, like sound, is undulatory, i.e. wave-like in its movements. Yet, by another analogy, light can be inferred to be not undulatory but vibrational. And physicists have not yet, as a matter of fact, made up their minds whether light is waves in motion or particles in motion.

Scientific Concepts

In our discussion of the scientific method thus far we have used the terms *cause, effect, condition*. A cause, we have seen by implication, is anything that contributes in any positive way to the existence or happening of something else. An effect, anything produced by a given cause. (The flying bullet caused the death of the fleeing deer.) A condition may be defined as anything which enables a cause to produce its effect without actually contributing toward the production itself. (The flying bullet caused the death of the fleeing deer, because the hunter was there to shoot the bullet.) A condition is not to be confused with an *occasion*, which may be defined as anything that occasions (not enables or determines) a cause to produce its effect. (The flying bullet caused the death of the fleeing deer, because the hunting season was on.) The effect *can* be without the occasion but *cannot* be without the condition.

Given causes, effects, and conditions, the scientific mind, observing, experimenting, making analogies, moves on to hypotheses, laws, theories. The *hypothesis*, the *law*, the *theory* must now be discussed as scientific concepts.

Hypothesis: An hypothesis is a generalization concerning the behavior of the physical world based upon observation and/or minimal experimentation. It is, as far as the scientific method is concerned, a starting point, a preconceived notion, a principle suggested.

Law: A law is an hypothesis which has been satisfactorily verified by experimentation. An hypothesis once proposed, experiments are conceived and conducted for the purpose of verifying the generalization. When due satisfaction is reached, by virtue of the specifically designed and planned experiments, the hypothesis becomes a law.

Theory: A theory is the explanation of the operation of a law or laws. A law or laws once discovered, the mind of the scientist, proceeding deductively, asks: what expressions concerning the behavior of the physical world can be deduced and stated in words or mathematical form which *explain* the operation of the law or laws?

The progression from observation of effects, conditions, causes, through experimentation, hypothesis, law, theory is pointedly seen in the steps followed by the famous British scientist of the nineteenth century, John Dalton, in arriving at his Atomic Theory.

The Scientific Method at Work

Dalton, observing that analyses of various substances always gave the same *numerical* values, independent of the source of the substance (whether occurring in nature or prepared by the chemist under various experimental conditions), conceived the idea that the proportions of the ingredients of a substance (oxygen and hydrogen in water, for example) were fixed, or constant, independent of the mode of its preparation. Thus was conceived the *hypothesis* regarding the *constancy of ratio* of analyzable components of a substance.

His curiosity thus aroused, Dalton embarked upon a careful and systematic investigation based on scientific experimentation designed to verify his idea. Could a given substance be prepared in which the ratios of the ingredients varied? The experiments of Dalton as well as those of other chemists altered the original hypothesis, but the idea itself was in no way discredited. And thus was evolved the *Law of Definite Proportions;* viz., the ratio of the ingredients of a given substance is a constant quantity, independent of its source or the manner of its preparation. In addition, Dalton formulated other laws concerning the structure of matter: the *Law of Multiple Proportions* and the *Law of Reciprocal Proportions*.

What, now, could be stated about matter which would explain the operation of these laws? was Dalton's next question. Given the laws, Dalton reasoned by deduction that matter was composed discontinuously of fundamental building units which he termed *atoms*. Thus, from the laws, was developed the *Atomic Theory* of matter, the postulation of which *explained* the operation of the laws themselves.

SUPPLEMENTARY READINGS FOR CHAPTER XII

Aristotle, *Analytica Posteriora*, 99b 20 - 100b 18.

Asher, M., "The Principle of Induction," *The Journal of Philosophy*, vol. 49, (November, 1952), pp. 741-747.

Bacon, F., *Advancement of Learning and Novum Organum*, rev. ed., Colonial Press, London, 1900.

Benjamin, A. C., "The Logical Structure of Science," *An Introduction to the Philosophy of Science*, The Macmillan Co., New York, 1937, pp. 41-60.

―――――, *An Introduction to the Philosophy of Science*, The Macmillan Co., New York, 1937, pp. 173-230.

Bloomfield, L., *Linguistic Aspects of Science*, "International Encyclopedia of United Science," vol. 1, No. 4, University of Chicago Press, Chicago, 1947.

Bridgman, P. W., "The Logic of Modern Physics," *Readings in the Philosophy of Science*, Feigl, H., and Brodbeck, M., Appleton-Century-Crofts, New York, 1953, pp. 34-46.

Buchdahl, G., "Induction and Scientific Method," *Mind*, vol. 60, (January, 1951), pp. 16-34.

Burks, A. W., "The Presupposition Theory of Induction," *Philosophy of Science*, vol. 20, 1953, pp. 177-197.

Carmichael, P. A., "The Metaphysical Matrix of Science," *Philosophy of Science*, vol. 20, 1953, pp. 208-216.

Carnap, R., "On Inductive Logic," *Philosophy of Science*, vol. 12, 1945, pp. 72-97.

————, "The Two Concepts of Probability," *Philosophy and Phenomenological Research*, vol. 5, (June, 1945), pp. 513-532.

————, "Remarks on Induction and Truth," *Philosophy and Phenomenological Research*, vol. 6, (June, 1946), pp. 590-602.

————, "What Is Probability," *Scientific American*, vol. 189, (September, 1953), pp. 128-138.

Chatalian, G., "Induction and the Problem of the External World," *Journal of Philosophy*, vol. 49, (September, 1952), pp. 601-607.

Churchman, C. W., "A Critique of Scientific Critiques," *The Review of Metaphysics*, vol. 7, No. 1, (September, 1953), pp. 89-97.

Chwistek, L., *The Limits of Science: Outline of Logic and the Methodology of the Exact Sciences*, Harcourt, Brace and Co., New York, 1949.

Clark, J. T., "Contemporary Science and Deductive Methodology," *Proceedings of the American Catholic Philosophical Association*, vol. 26, 1952, pp. 94-131.

Coffey, B., "Philosophy of Science and the Scientific Attitude," *The Modern Schoolman*, vol. 26, (May, 1949), pp. 331-336.

Cohen, M. R., and Nagel E., *An Introduction to Logic and Scientific Method*, Harcourt, Brace and Co., New York, 1934, Chap. 14, pp. 273-288.

————, *An Introduction to Logic and Scientific Method*, Harcourt, Brace and Co., New York, 1934, Chap. 17, 18, pp. 323-375.

Dotterer, R. H., "Ignorance and Equal Probability," *Philosophy of Science*, vol. 8, 1941, pp. 297-303.

Dubs, H. H., *Rational Induction*, University of Chicago Press, Chicago, Illinois, 1930.

Ducasse, C. J., "Bacon's Philosophy of Science," *Structure, Method, and Meaning*: Essays in Honor of Henry M. Sheffer, ed. Henle, P., Kallen, H. M., Langer, S. K., New York, Liberal Arts Press, 1951, pp. 115-144.

Feigl, H., "The Logical Character of the Principle of Induction," *Readings in Philosophical Analysis*, Appleton-Century-Crofts, New York, 1949, pp. 297-304.

Feigl, H., "Some remarks on the Meaning of Scientific Explanation," *Readings in Philosophical Analysis,* Appleton-Century-Crofts, New York, 1949, pp. 510-514.

Greenwood, T., "Euclid and Aristotle," *The Thomist,* vol. 15, (July, 1952), pp. 374-403.

Harrod, H. R. F., "Induction and Probability," *Philosophy,* vol. 26, 1951, pp. 37-52.

Hempel, C. G., "On the Nature of Mathematical Truth," *Readings in Philosophical Analysis,* Appleton-Century-Crofts, New York, 1949, pp. 222-237.

Hofstadter, A., "Causality and Necessity," *Journal of Philosophy,* vol. 46, (April, 1949), pp. 257-270.

Huntington, E. V., "The Method of Postulates," *Philosophy of Science,* vol. 4, 1937, pp. 482-495.

Kane, Corcoran, Ashley, Nogar, "The Problem of Induction of Principles," *Science in Synthesis,* Albertus Magnus Lyceum for Natural Science, Dominican College of St. Thomas Aquinas, River Forest, Illinois, 1952, pp. 136-141.

Kapp, E., *Greek Foundations of Traditional Logic,* Columbia University Press, New York, 1942, pp. 75-87.

Kaufmann, F., *Methodology of the Social Sciences,* New York, Oxford University Press, 1944.

————, "On the Nature of Inductive Inference," *Philosophy and Phenomenological Research,* vol. 6, (June, 1946), pp. 602-609.

Keynes, J. N., *A Treatise on Probability,* Macmillan, London, 1921.

Kneale, W., *Probability and Induction,* The Clarendon Press, Oxford, 1949, pp. 92-110.

Knight, F. H., "The Limitations of Scientific Method in Economics," *The Trend of Economics,* ed. Tugwell, R., New York, 1924, pp. 229-267.

Kocourek, R. A., Schorsch, A., "Nature of Induction and Scientific Induction," *Proceedings of the American Catholic Philosophical Association,* vol. 25, 1951, pp. 130-141.

Maritain, J., "The Conflict of Methods at the End of the Middle Ages," *The Thomist,* vol. 3, No. 4, 1941, pp. 527-538.

McWilliams, J. A., "Cause in Science and in Philosophy," *The Modern Schoolman,* vol. 25, (November, 1947), pp. 11-18.

Menger, K., "Postulational Method," *The Modern Schoolman*, vol. 25, (March, 1948), pp. 190-192.

Mill, J. S., *A System of Logic*, J. W. Parker, London, 1851.

Nicod, J., "The Logical Problem of Induction," *Foundations of Geometry and Induction*, The Humanities Press, New York, 1950, pp. 197-281.

Reichenback, H., "On the Justification of Induction," *Journal of Philosophy*, vol. 37, (February, 1940), pp. 97-103.

Ritchie, A. D., *Scientific Method*, Harcourt, Brace and Co., New York, 1923.

Schorsch, A., "Scientific Induction," *Proceedings of the American Catholic Philosophical Association*, vol. 25, 1951, pp. 136-141.

Smith, M., "The Method of Elimination in Scientific Study," *Philosophy of Science*, vol. 10, 1943, pp. 250-254.

Smith, V. E., "Abstraction and the Empiriological Method," *Proceedings of the American Catholic Philosophical Association*, vol. 26, 1952, pp. 35-50.

Spilsbury, R. J., "A Note on Induction," *Mind*, vol. 58, (April, 1949), pp. 215-217.

Strawson, P. F., *Introduction to Logical Theory*, John Wiley & Sons, Inc., New York, 1952, pp. 248-263.

Sullivan, Sister H., O.S.B., *An Introduction to the Philosophy of Natural and Mathematical Sciences*, Vantage Press, New York, 1952.

Thomas Aquinas, *The Division and Methods of the Sciences*, trans. A. Maurer, C.S.B., Pontifical Institute of Medieval Studies, Toronto, 1953.

Ushenko, A. P., "The Problem of Causal Inference," *Philosophy of Science*, vol. 9, 1942, pp. 132-138.

Veatch, H. B., *Intentional Logic*, Yale University Press, New Haven, 1952, pp. 316-331.

Von Wright, G. H., "On Probability," *Mind*, vol. 49, (July, 1940), pp. 265-283.

―――――, *The Logical Problem of Induction*, Soc. Philosophica, Helsinki, 1941.

Walcott, G. D., *Logic and Scientific Method*, Edwards Brothers, Inc., Ann Arbor, Michigan, 1952.

Walker, E. R., "Verification and Probability," *Journal of Philosophy*, vol. 44, (February, 1947), pp. 97-104.

Wang, H., "On the Justification of Induction," *Journal of Philosophy*, vol. 44, (December, 1947), pp. 701-710.

Weaver, W., "Fundamental Questions in Science," *Scientific American*, vol. 189, (September, 1953), pp. 47-51.

Westaway, F. W., *Scientific Method*, Blackie and Son, Glasgow, 1912.

Wightman, W. P. D., *The Growth of Scientific Ideas*, Yale University Press, New Haven, 1951.

Wilson, J. C., *Statement and Inference*, The Clarendon Press, Oxford, vol. II, 1926, pp. 578-662.

Wolf, A., *Essentials of Scientific Method*, G. Allen, London, 1928.

CHAPTER XIII

The Old and The New

To the Student, an Explanation

In logic, as in other branches of philosophy, as in political economy, sociology, art, literature, music, as indeed in almost all man's practical, intellectual, and spiritual concerns, the modern era has seen in many quarters a turning away from the past, from what has gone before — as old, outmoded, false, "a dead time's exploded dream." How to account for this restlessness of modern times, this dissatisfaction with the old, this craving for the new (if only, sometimes, because it is new) is a question that has troubled many minds great and small, that has brought forth many theories sensible and nonsensical, and that, in the last analysis, is properly the concern not of the history of philosophy but of the philosophy of history.

Nevertheless, the student unquestionably has encountered (if only by implication) in his supplementary readings some idea of the dichotomy that exists in the minds of some between the so-called "old logic" and the so-called "new logic." It is the purpose of this chapter, as far as it is possible in a book of this kind, first, to bring to the student some understanding of this division among contemporary logicians and of the concomitant problems of "semantics" and "the logical paradox" and second, to show him a) that the so-called new logic in no way discredits the so-called old, b) that there are really not two logics at all but one, begun in antiquity and continuing, as part of the very nature of man, to this very moment.

Traditional Logic

When reference is made to the "old" or "traditional" logic, what is meant is the logic of Aristotle, founded by him in the glory of Greek antiquity, interpreted, propounded in the Middle Ages by St. Thomas Aquinas, and through his followers, Duns Scotus, William of Ockham, and others (the great thinkers of the Scholastic tradition), handed down through the centuries to modern times. It is the logic properly called *Aristotelian, Thomistic, Scholastic.* It is the logic of Parts One, Two, and Three of this book.

No small hope, is it, on the part of the present writers that the logic of Aristotle, Aquinas, and the Scholastic tradition by now sits well with the student. Futile the expense of energy on their part and, to be sure, on the part of the instructor, if it does not. But let it be said here that this so-called traditional logic does not sit well with everybody at the present time. In not a few of the non-sectarian colleges and universities of the land traditional logic is relegated to the category of a dead science or a quaint historical curiosity. In not a few quarters the charge is leveled against it that it takes little account of modern developments in the field. Even among upholders of the tradition there is voiced a recognition "of the undeveloped state of the logic of Aristotle and St. Thomas which therefore needs completion."[4] What, then, is to be made of this state of affairs? The answer to this question, it is hoped, will be made clear by what follows in the remainder of the present chapter.

The New Logic

The so-called new logic goes under a variety of names; it is refered to as *symbolic, mathematical, algorithmic.* Sometimes it is called simply *logistics,* sometimes *the algebra of logic,* sometimes *the logic of pure form.* It represents a calculated attempt to replace the traditional logic of terms and propositions, or of concepts and judgments, by a system of "signs" or "symbols" conceived as being related in the way that the elements of algebra or, more generally, of mathematics are related — for the purpose of achieving a logic of "wider meaning". It represents, to put it another way, the attempt to systematize by symbolization man's knowledge about his thoughts. More specifically, it is concerned with studying the relation between mathematics and logic, with reducing logic to axioms after the pattern of mathematics, and with developing mathematics from logic.

What motivates this attempt is the notion that the Aristotelian logic of terms and propositions (the *logic of words*) is *restricting*, by reason of its being tied to meaning, and *shifting*, by reason of the vagaries of language, and that by means of a mathematical logic we might better explore "the hidden anatomy of human reason" for the purpose of revealing "the amazing extent of its latent powers."[5]

What is the stand of traditional logic, now, in the face of this attempt and the notions which motivate it? To begin with, the notion that "symbolic" logic is something new and divorced from the traditional is misleading. Much of the work of modern symbolic logicians was anticipated by the logicians in the Scholastic tradition and has parallels in their logical systems.[6] Aristotle himself was the first to acknowledge the function of symbols in logic. "It is impossible," he said, "in a discussion to bring in the actual things discussed: we use their names as symbols instead of them; and therefore we suppose that what follows in the names, follows in the things as well, just as people who calculate suppose in regard to their counters."[7]

The importance of symbolization as a scientific method of accuracy no one who understands the meaning of "science" and "accuracy" can deny. But when symbolization becomes, in effect, an end in itself, when it becomes "the realization of the ideal of logic, the exhibition of form,"[8] when form becomes disassociated with matter to the point of ignoring if not denying matter, then meaning itself becomes meaningless — and no logic is right and none is wrong, and logic itself is the figment of a figment in a dream. When symbolism becomes wrapped up in itself it loses contact with reality, a condition that in psychiatry falls into the classification of a disease. A mathematical logic or a logic of pure form becomes, in the end, a denial of the correlation of sensory knowledge and intelligible knowledge. And Aristotle's dictum that *sensation is of the singular but its content is universal,* which gives meaning to man's rational life, becomes mere wordage, indeed mere form devoid itself of meaning.

Lastly, let it be admitted that the logic of Aristotle is incomplete. But let the manner in which it is incomplete also be admitted. If the purpose of logic be the systematization (or *symbolization*) of knowledge, it is to be noted that this is precisely what is to be found in Aristotle's theory of mediate inferences. What remains to be done, and what is being done by those who realize the need, is the *symbolization* of Aristotle's logic of terms and propositions — a logic not of form only, but of form and content. The true logician, then, will not turn in upon himself in the face of modern logic but will look to the new for what it may contain, good and valid, that may be used in this work of completion.

From the foregoing it should be apparent that a symbolic logic, rightly understood for what it is and for the purpose it is intended to serve, is not only possible but practicable. Symbolic logic thus understood, however, comes within the province not of the beginning student but of the advanced one, and as part of the academic curriculum it is frequently not met of thought. He holds that a word or term is the sign of an idea, and that the idea in the word is identical with the truth in the thing. He believes that the logical connection between the symbol function of a term and its meaning function is a reflection of the connection between knowledge and reality. He believes that the most important relation to be considered in the use of words is the relation between the mind and the thing. He believes, in short, that the function of language is to report, as truly as possible, on reality. He believes, finally, that he has and that traditional logic has always had its semantics, which can be stated very briefly: *Terms (or words) are conventional signs (or symbols) of ideas or concepts; concepts are the formal signs of things.*[11] This understood, the purpose of language may thus be said to be to aid logic in bringing to the mind an exact, orderly, and true knowledge of things or reality.

Out of this grows the conviction that what is needed by the logician, in regard to his concern over the interplay of language and logic, is:

1) An awareness that language *is* arbitrary, that it matters little whether we all agree to call *hat* not hat but *shoe*, as long as we all know and agree upon what *hat-ness* is.

2) An awareness that, although language is shifting and significations as a result are likewise frequently shifting, *meanings* (the things signified) do not shift.

3) A knowledge of his particular language, of its history and development, of its syntactical structure, of its vocabulary, of its levels of usage, of the difference between denotative and connotative significations of its words.

4) A courage to face the onerous fact that the true thinker must be both logician and grammarian.

Paradox

The problem of the logical paradox is not so much a point of departure separating the old from the new as it is a concern which intrigues, if not disturbs, the new more than the old. The paradox has been with the science of logic from its very beginnings. Indeed, some of the Greek thinkers made a veritable science of it. To the medievalist it was an *insoluble*, a thing which could not be explained or which man could not yet understand. To many a modernist it is a serious problem which threatens the foundations not only of logic but perhaps of science itself.

The logical paradox might be defined as 1) a proposition which is both true and false at the same time, 2) a group of propositions which simultaneously affirm and deny one another. Thus, if an American were to say *All Americans are liars*, he himself being included among the liars, the proposition could be true and false at the same time. And if this be the case, we seem to face a denial of the Law of Contradiction (a proposition cannot be true and false at the same time). The classic example (somewhat modified) of the second type might be put this way:

Smith: What Jones is about to say is false.

Jones: Smith has just spoken the truth.

These and other forms of paradox, which are merely variations of the two types given, are not contradictions, refutations, or denials of any of the fundamental principles upon which the science of logic rests. They are, in effect, the mind playing tricks upon itself. The perpetual motion machine, the image of the two snakes swallowing each other, the eye within the eye within the eye of Dali, the box within the box within the box on the cornflakes wrapper — is the mind to despair of thought, of the true and the false, in the light of these?

Rightly seen, the logical paradox explodes itself in the face of the *doctrine of supposition over and above signification*.[12] Thus *All Americans are liars* is true or false depending upon whether "all Americans" supposes "all other Americans" and/or "liars" supposes "people who sometimes do not speak truth", and so on. Further, if Smith has just spoken the truth by saying, "What Jones is about to say is false," both propositions are true or false depending upon whether "the truth" supposes the proposition "What Jones is about to say is false" or "that which Jones was about to say," and so on. The customary example in symbolic logic of the simultaneous truth of *The cat is drinking milk* and *the cat is not drinking milk,* in which "cat" in the first instance supposes the *animal* and in the second instance supposes the *word,* depends upon the doctrine of supposition over and above signification.

The paradox, then, is not so much a problem as it is a trick. Indeed, in the hands of literary people it becomes an effective device, not to obscure truth but to lay it bare. "Nothing fails like success," says Chesterton, in a paradox that is not a paradox at all but an incisive glimpse into a truth most men learn too late.

SUPPLEMENTARY READINGS FOR CHAPTER XIII

Anderson, F. H., *The Philosophy of Francis Bacon,* University of Chicago Press, Chicago, Illinois, 1948, pp. 217-258.

Ardley, G., "The Logic of the Categorical," *Aquinas and Kant,* Longmans, Green and Co., 1950, pp. 114-124.

Avey, A. E., "Recent Schools of Logic," *A History of Philosophical Systems,* ed. V. Ferm, The Philosophical Library, New York, 1950, pp. 504-515.

Bentley, A. F., "Logicians' Underlying Postulations," *Philosophy of Science,* vol. 13, 1946, pp. 3-19.

Bergmann, G., "Semantics," *A History of Philosophical Systems*, ed. V. Ferm, The Philosophical Library, New York, 1950, pp. 483-492.

Bochenski, I. M., "On Analogy," *The Thomist*, vol. 11, No. 4, 1948, pp. 424-447.

————, "On the Syntactical Categories," *The New Scholasticism*, vol. 23, 1949, pp. 257-280.

————, *Ancient Formal Logic*, North Holland Publishing Co., Amsterdam, 1951, The Humanities Press, New York.

Boehner, P., "De Insolubili," *Medieval Logic*, University of Chicago Press, Chicago, 1952, pp. 12-14.

Boole, G., *The Mathematical Analysis of Logic*, Philosophical Library, New York, 1949.

Brady, I., "The New Aristotle," *The New Scholasticism*, vol. 27, 1953, pp. 305-334.

Carnap, R., *Introduction to Semantics*, Harvard University Press, Cambridge, 1942.

Church, A., "Logic: Formal, Symbolic, Traditional," *Dictionary of Philosophy*, Philosophical Library, New York, pp. 170-182.

Churchman, C. W., "The Logical Paradoxes," *Elements of Logic and Formal Science*, J. B. Lippincott Co., New York, 1940, pp. 197-216.

Clark, J. T., *Conventional Logic and Modern Logic*, Woodstock College Press, Woodstock, Maryland, 1952, pp. 1-60.

Cooley, J. C., *A Primer of Formal Logic*, The Macmillan Co., New York, 1942.

Copleston, F. C., "Philosophy and Language," *Month*, vol. 197, (May, 1951), pp. 270-278.

Couturat, L., *The Algebra of Logic*, Open Court Co., Chicago, 1914.

Cunningham, G. W., "The New Logic and the Old," *Journal of Philosophy*, vol. 36, (October, 1939), pp. 565-572.

De Morgan, A., *Formal Logic*, Taylor and Walton, London, 1847.

Dűrr, K., *The Propositional Logic of Boethius*, North Holland Publishing Co., Amsterdam, 1951, The Humanities Press, New York.

Eaton, R. M., *General Logic*, Scribner's Sons, New York, 1931, pp. 359-477.

Enriques, F., *The Historic Development of Logic*, tr. from Italian by Jerome Rosenthal, Henry Holt Co., New York, 1929.

Evans, I., "Words and Meanings," *Blackfriars*, vol. 28, (August, 1947), pp. 367-370.

Farber, M., "Logical Systems and the Principles of Logic," *Philosophy of Science*, vol. 9, 1942, pp. 40-54.

Feibleman, J. K., "How to Read a Word," *Philosophy and Phenomenological Research*, vol. 3, (June, 1943), pp. 478-486.

Frege, G., *Philosophical Writings*, The Philosophical Library, New York, 1953.

Geach, P., and Black, M., *Translations from the Philosophical Writings of Gottlob Frege*, The Philosophical Library, New York, 1952.

Gray, L. H., *Foundations of Language*, The Macmillan Company, New York, 1939.

Greenwood, T., "Plato and Aristotle: A Contrast Between their Mathematical Outlook," *The New Scholasticism*, vol. 18, 1944, pp. 262-269.

————, "The Unity of Logic," *The Thomist*, vol. 8, No. 4, 1945, pp. 457-470.

Herberg, W., "Semantic Corruption," *Catholic Mind*, vol. 44, (February, 1946), pp. 95-101.

Hess, M. W., "Language and Sense Perfection," *The Thomist*, vol. 10, (January, 1947), pp. 56-74.

————, "Cult of Verbal Noises," *Catholic World*, vol. 165, (June, 1947), pp. 256-259.

————, "Semantic Question," *The New Scholasticism*, vol. 23, 1949, pp. 186-206.

Hofstadter, A., "On Semantic Problems," *Journal of Philosophy*, vol. 35, (April, 1938), pp. 225-232.

Joseph, H. W. B., "Logic and Mathematics," *Philosophy*, vol. 3, 1928, pp. 3-14.

Kane, Corcoran, Ashley, Nogar, "Modern Logic and Ancient Problems," *Science in Synthesis*, Albertus Magnus Lyceum for Natural Science, Dominican College of St. Thomas Aquinas, River Forest, Illinois, 1952, pp. 83-86.

Kattsoff, L. O., "The Place of Logic in a World of Fact," *Philophy and Phenomenological Research*, vol. 10, (September, 1949), pp. 121-129.

Kelly, A. D., "Some Aspects of the 'New Logic'," *Philosophy*, vol. 7, 1932, pp. 461-466.

King, H. R., "Aristotle and the Paradoxes of Zeno," *Journal of Philosophy*, vol. 46, (October, 1949), pp. 657-670.

Kneale, W., "Boole and the Revival of Logic," *Mind*, vol. 57, (April, 1948), pp. 149-175.

Kocourek, R. A., "An Evaluation of Symbolic Logic," *Proceedings of the American Catholic Philosophical Association*, vol. 22, 1947, pp. 95-104.

Korzybski, A., *Science and Sanity*, International Non-Aristotelian Library Publishing Company, Lancaster, Pa., 1945.

Langford, C. H., "The Paradoxes," *Journal of Philosophy*, vol. 47, (December, 1950), pp. 777-778.

Larguier, E. H., "A Theory of Mathematical Reality," *The Modern Schoolman*, vol. 16, No. 4, 1939, pp. 88-91.

————, "Concerning Some Views on the Structure of Mathematics," *The Thomist*, vol. 4, No. 3, 1942, pp. 431-445.

Leblanc, H., "The Semiotic Function of Predicates," *Journal of Philosophy*, vol. 46, (December, 1949), pp. 838-844.

LeBlond, J., "Cartesian Method and Classical Logic," *The Modern Schoolman*, vol. 15, No. 1, 1937, pp. 4-6.

Lewis, C. I., *Survey of Symbolic Logic*, University of California Press, Berkeley, 1918.

————, "Notes on the Logic of Intension," *Structure, Method, and Meaning: Essays in Honor of Henry M. Sheffer*, Liberal Arts Press, New York, 1951, pp. 25-34.

Mates, B., *Stoic Logic*, University of California Press, Berkeley and Los Angeles, 1953.

Menger, K., "The New Logic," *Philosophy of Science*, vol. 4, 1937, pp. 299-336.

Mesthene, E. G., "On the Status of the Laws of Logic," *Philosophy and Phenomenological Research*, vol. 10, (March, 1950), pp. 354-373.

Miller, J. W., *The Structure of Aristotelian Logic*, Kegan Paul, Trench, Trubner Co. Ltd., London, 1938.

Montague, W. P., "The Modern Distemper of Philosophy," *Journal of Philosophy*, vol. 48, (July, 1951), pp. 429-435.

Moody, E. A., *Truth and Consequence in Medieval Logic*, North-Holland Publishing Co., Amsterdam, 1953, The Humanities Press, New York.

Nagel, E., "Some Theses in the Philosophy of Logic," *Philosophy of Science*, vol. 5, 1938, pp. 46-51.

Oesterle, J. A., Review of *Intentional Logic*, Henry Babcock Veatch, Yale University Press, New Haven, 1952, *The Thomist*, vol. 16, (July, 1953), pp. 413-425.

O'Grady, D. C., "Mathematics and Philosophy," *The New Scholasticism*, vol. 6, 1932, pp. 120-129.

O'Neill, J. M., "Semantics and Responsibility," *Catholic Library World*, vol. 24, (October, 1952), pp. 5-10.

Philipov, A., *Logic and Dialectic in the Soviet Union*, Research Program on the U.S.S.R., New York, 1952.

Post, E. L., "Introduction to a General Theory of Elementary Propositions," *American Journal of Mathematics*, vol. 43, 1921, pp. 163-185.

Prior, A. N., *Logic and the Basis of Ethics*, Oxford University Press, London, 1946.

————, "The Parva Logicalia in Modern Dress," *Dominican Studies*, vol. 5, 1952, pp. 78-87.

————, "The Logic of Negative Terms in Boethius, *Franciscan Studies*, vol. 13, 1953, pp. 1-6.

————, "On Some Consequentiae in Walter Burleigh," *The New Scholasticism*, vol. 27, 1953, pp. 433-446.

Quine, W. V., "Completeness of the Propositional Calculus," *The Journal of Symbolic Logic*, vol. 3, 1938, pp. 37-40.

————, *From a Logical Point of View; Logico – Philosophical Essays*, Harvard University Press, Cambridge, 1953.

Ritchie, A. D., "A Defense of Aristotle's Logic," *Mind*, vol. 55, (July, 1946), pp. 256-262.

Ritter, W. E., "Logic in Our Common Knowledge," *Philosophy of Science*, vol. 11, 1944, pp. 59-81.

Rooney, M., "Law and the New Logic," *Proceedings of the American Catholic Philosophical Association*, vol. 16, 1940, pp. 192-222.

Rosenbloom, P., *The Elements of Mathematical Logic*, Dover Publications, Inc., New York, 1951.

Rougier, L., "The Relativity of Logic," *Philosophy and Phenomenological Research*, vol. 2, (December, 1941), pp. 137-157.

Sabine, G. H., "Logic and the Social Studies," *The Philosophical Review*, vol. 48, 1939, pp. 155-176.

Searles, H. L., *Logic and Scientific Method*, The Ronald Press, New York, 1948.

Singer, M. C., "Formal Logic and Dewey's Logic," *The Philosophical Review*, vol. 60, 1951, pp. 375-385.

Smith, V. E., "Dr. Charles Morris and Semiotic," *The Modern Schoolman*, vol. 25, (January, 1948), pp. 140-143.

Strawson, P. F., *Introduction to Logical Theory*, John Wiley & Sons, Inc., New York, 1952, pp. 211-232.

Sutfin, E., "Bacon's Opinion of His Predecessors," *The New Scholasticism*, vol. 18, 1944, pp. 147-184.

Taliaferro, R. C., "Plato and the Liberal Arts: A Plea for Mathematical Logic," *The New Scholasticism*, vol. 11, 1937, pp. 297-319.

Thomas, I., "Logic and Theology," *Dominican Studies*, vol. 1, 1948, pp. 291-312.

———, "Introductory Remarks to Modern Logic," *Blackfriars*, vol. 33, (July-August, 1952), pp. 299-305.

Thompson, M. H., "The Logical Paradoxes and Peirce's Semiotic," *Journal of Philosophy*, vol. 46, (August, 1949), pp. 513-536.

Ushenko, A. P., *The Problems of Logic*, Princeton University Press, Princeton, 1941.

———, "A Note on the Semantic Conception of Truth," *Philosophy and Phenomenological Research*, vol. 5, (September, 1944), pp. 104-107.

Veatch, H., "Concerning the Ontological Status of Logical Forms," *The Review of Metaphysics*, vol. 2, No. 6, 1948, pp. 40-64.

———, "Aristotelian and Mathematical Logic," *The Thomist*, vol. 13, No. 1, (January, 1950), pp. 50-96.

———, "Basic Confusions in Current Notions of Propositional Calculi," *The Thomist*, vol. 14, 1951, pp. 238-258.

Veatch, H., and Young, T., "Metaphysics and the Paradoxes," *The Review of Metaphysics*, vol. 6, (December, 1952), pp. 199-218.

Veatch, H., *Intentional Logic*, Yale University Press, New Haven, 1952, pp. 29-76.
————, *Intentional Logic*, Yale University Press, New Haven, 1952, pp. 115-153.
————, *Intentional Logic*, Yale University Press, New Haven, 1952, pp. 213-229.
————, *Intentional Logic*, Yale University Press, New Haven, 1952, pp. 344-358.
Venn, J., *The Principles of Empirical or Inductive Logic*, Macmillan & Co., London, 1889.
Walpole, H. R., *Semantics*, W. W. Norton & Co., Inc., New York, 1941.
Walsh, F. A., "The Theory of Fallacy in Aristotle and Kant," *The New Scholasticism*, vol. 2, 1928, pp. 357-366.
Wellmuth, J. J., "Philosophy and Order in Logic," *Proceedings of the American Catholic Philosophical Association*, vol. 17, 1941, pp. 12-18.
————, "Some Comments on the Nature of Mathematical Logic," *The New Scholasticism*, vol. 16, 1942, pp. 9-15.
Whitehead, A. N., and Russel, B., *Principia Mathematica*, 2nd ed., Cambridge University Press, Cambridge, 1925-27.
Whittaker, J. F., "The Position of Mathematics in the Hierarchy of Speculative Science," *The Thomist*, vol. 3, (July, 1941), pp. 467-506.
Wick, W. A., *Metaphysics and the New Logic*, University of Chicago Press, Chicago, 1942.
Wittgenstein, L., *Tractatus Logico-Philosophicus*, Harcourt, Brace and Co., New York, 1933.

CHAPTER XIV

Logical Positivism

Again, Preliminaries to a Definition

Reference was made in Chapter XII to the "method" of "naturalism", "logical empiricism", or "logical positivism" as distinct from the *scientific method* there discussed. What is behind this distinction it is the purpose of this chapter to make clear. There is a species or system of logic, not unrelated to symbolism and semantics, which goes under the name of *logical positivism*. Logical positivism is based upon the philosophy of "naturalism" and upon the concept of "scientific enterprise" by reason of which it ties in with science and the scientific method in general and is, in fact, not infrequently identified with the latter.

The philosophy of *naturalism* is not something to be explained in hard and fast terms, and naturalists themselves in our day are by no means in complete agreement with one another as to the principles, views, beliefs which are supposed to bind them together under the name which they themselves have given to their school. In the space available here it can be said that naturalism is a philosophy based essentially on a rejection of the traditional view of the duality of reality, in the sense of a distinction between the natural order and the supernatural order, between matter and spirit. Indeed, it is not a philosophy at all but a *science* "that insists on the importance and reality of all man's experience and enterprises, and has developed concepts that promise to render them all intelligible," in consequence of which man is able to erect for himself "philosophies that can find a natural and intelligible place for all human interests and aims, and can embrace in one natural world, amenable to a single intellectual method, all the realities to which human experience points . . ."[13] Further, in the words again of the naturalist himself:

> In its fundamental attitude, in its basic metaphysical position, contemporary naturalism is thus back once more with the naturalistic world-view of the Greeks. But it has increased its resources to include all that men have learned since the ancients. It now possesses in great detail a knowledge of the structures or ways of behaving of things, and the elaborate set of techniques and standards of inquiry and verification that constitute the scientific enterprise, the most potent instrument the wit of man has yet devised for analysis and control. For it, man is still what he was for the Greeks, an intelligent and valuing animal living in an intelligible and valuable world. He now knows something about the nature of that world, and is beginning to learn how to make it serve his ends.[14]

For the naturalist *truth* thus becomes "the discernment of the systematic, structural aspect of Nature, which conditions the appearance of events and can be used as the means to human ends." Good becomes "the system of valuable aspects of Nature, the organization of experienced goods into a reasonably harmonious whole."[15]

From this limited monistic view of man's knowledge, which centers all the possibilities of truth exclusively in matter and dismisses (either by denial or by doubt) the spirit, derives the notion of *scientific enterprise*, as already noted, and its corollary, scientific *empiricism*. Empiricism, as used by the naturalist, suggests knowledge based exclusively upon the scientific method; that is to say, upon inductive inference, using deduction only to the extent that it instigates and directs induction. More specifically, it suggests the acceptance of only those propositions that are testable and confirmable. In the case of particulars the testability and confirmability must be complete; in the case of universals it need not be.[16]

And Now, The Definition

Logical positivism is most frequently defined as a "system which excludes everything but the natural phenomena or properties of knowable things, together with their relations of coexistence and succession." Following the theories of Auguste Comte (1798-1857), it holds that the only valid knowledge is knowledge of facts, that certitude lies exclusively in the experimental sciences, that the mind cannot attain to essences but grasps only facts and relations of facts, that the mind escapes error only if it renounces *a priori* notions and adheres to experience. Its emphasis is, then, upon physicalism. Its goal is the unity of scientific knowledge, "a single intellectual method," the development of a set of universal, fundamental laws from which all the special laws of the sciences can be deduced. It stresses symbolism, a comprehensive theory of signs as a means to its end, for which indeed it invents a name: *semiotic*. The logic based on this system, then, is what is meant by *logical positivism*.

The Limitations of Logical Positivism

Because it is monistic in its view, because it centers all the possibilities of truth exclusively in matter, because it dismisses the spirit, because it admits only those propositions that are scientifically testable and confirmable, because it denies to the mind attainability of essences and exalts the knowability of the coexistence and succession of natural phenomena or properties of "knowable things," because, in brief, it renounces *a priori* concepts — logical positivism is obviously a limited system of thought. It represents, in fact, a deliberate and systematic narrowing of man's intellectual horizons. It represents an attempt to reduce spirit to matter, concepts to phantasms, and intellection to a description of sensory phenomena. Thus, God as He has revealed Himself to us, the soul of man as we know it, the hope of salvation as we feel it, and reason as we use it to lift us from the level of pure sense are things that logical positivism doubts (agnosticism) or denies (atheism).

Logical Positivism and Traditional Logic

In opposition to logical positivism the logic of Scholasticism upholds the duality of reality, affirms the spirit, and declares the knowability of essences. Its view is "empirico-rational, inducto-deductive, and a *priori — a posteriori.*" It believes "that concepts are not reducible to percepts . . . and that judgment is not reducible to mere association." It avers that "the intellect does have what is called an extrinsic or objective dependence upon the senses, which provide the raw-material of experience from which by its process of abstraction it elaborates its universal concepts and then unites them in the act of judgment."[17]

Traditional logic does not deny the reaches of a logical positivism but it decries its restrictions. Believing in a higher kind of knowledge than mere sense perception, and taking up where logical positivism leaves off (at the level of the senses, the empirical, the *a posteriori*) the logic of Scholasticism moves on to the concept and the judgment (at the level of reason, the deductive, the *a priori*). Refusing to regard "sense and reason as totally disconnected or mutually antipathetic, the Thomistic system is the only school of thought which offers an account of their relationship, with abstraction as the key, that recognizes the legitimate claims of both levels of knowledge."[18]

SUPPLEMENTARY READINGS FOR CHAPTER XIV

Anderson, F. H., *The Philosophy of Francis Bacon*, University of Chicago Press, Chicago, 1948.

Ayer, A. J., *The Foundations of Empirical Knowledge*, The Macmillan Co., New York, 1940.

Barnes, W. H. F., "Is Philosophy Possible? A Study of Logical Positivism," *Philosophy*, vol. 22, 1947, pp. 25-48.

Benjamin, A. C., "Theories of Scientific Concepts," *An Introduction to the Philosophy of Science*, The Macmillan Co., New York, 1937, pp. 147-172.

Bentley, A. F., "The Positive and the Logical," *Philosophy of Science*, vol. 3, 1936, pp. 472-485.

Berenda, C. W., "A Five-Fold Skepticism in Logical Empiricism," *Philosophy of Science*, vol. 17, 1950, pp. 123-132.

Bergmann, G., "Logical Positivism," *A History of Philosophical Systems*, ed. V. Ferm, The Philosophical Library, New York, 1950, pp. 471-482.

———, "Outline of an Empiricist Philosophy of Physics," *Readings in the Philosophy of Science*, ed. H. Feigl, and M. Brodbeck, Appleton-Century-Crofts, Inc., New York, 1953, pp. 262-287.

Brodbeck, M. "The New Rationalism: Dewey's Theory of Intuition," *Journal of Philosophy*, vol. 46, (November, 1949), pp. 780-791.

Buchler, J., "Peirce's Theory of Logic," *Journal of Philosophy*, vol. 36, (April, 1939), pp. 197-215.

Cerf, W., "Logical Positivism and Existentialism," *Philosophy of Science*, vol. 18, 1951, pp. 327-338.

Chisholm, R. M., "Sextus Empiricus and Modern Empiricism," *Philosophy of Science*, vol. 8, 1941, pp. 371-384.

———, "The Problem of Empiricism," *Journal of Philosophy*, vol. 45, (September, 1948), pp. 512-517.

Connolly, F. G., "Science vs. Philosophy," *The Modern Schoolman*, vol. 29, No. 3, 1952, pp. 197-209.

Copleston, F., "Some Reflections on Logical Positivism," *Dublin Review*, vol. 224, No. 448, 1950, pp. 71-86.

Dawson, C., "The Origins of the European Scientific Tradition: St. Thomas and Roger Bacon," *Clergy Review*, vol. II, 1931, pp. 193-205.

Dewey, J., "Antinaturalism in Extremis," *Naturalism and the Human Spirit*, ed. Y. H. Krikorian, Columbia University Press, New York, 1944, pp. 1-16.

Farber, M., *Philosophic Thought in France and the United States*, University of Buffalo Publications in Philosophy, Buffalo, 1950, Part II.

Feibleman, J. K., "The Metaphysics of Logical Positivism," *The Review of Metaphysics*, vol. 5, 1951, pp. 55-82.

Feigl, H., "Logical Empiricism," *Readings in Philosophical Analysis*, Appleton-Century-Crofts, Inc., New York, 1949, pp. 3-23.

—————, "The Scientific Outlook: Naturalism and Humanism," *Readings in the Philosophy of Science*, ed. H. Feigl, and M. Brodbeck, Appleton-Century-Crofts, Inc., New York, 1953, pp. 8-18.

—————, "Operationism and Scientific Method," *Readings in Philosophical Analysis*, Appleton-Century-Crofts, Inc., New York, 1949, pp. 498-509.

Ferm, V., "Varieties of Naturalism," *A History of Philosophical Systems*, ed. V. Ferm, The Philosophical Library, New York, 1950, pp. 429-441.

Frank, P., "The Place of Logic and Metaphysics in the Advancement of Modern Science," *Philosophy of Science*, vol. 15, 1948, pp. 275-286.

—————, *Relativity — a Richer Truth*, Beacon Press, Boston, 1950.

Frankel, C., "Positivism," *A History of Philosophical Systems*, ed. V. Ferm, The Philosophical Library, New York, 1950, pp. 329-339.

Gallagher, D., "Contemporary Thomism," *A History of Philosophical Systems*, ed. V. Ferm, The Philosophical Library, New York, 1950, pp. 454-470.

Gallie, W. B., *Peirce and Pragmatism*, Penguin Books, Baltimore, 1952.

Garnett, A. C., "Must Empiricism Be Materialistic and Behavioristic?" *Journal of Philosophy*, vol. 47, (April, 1950), pp. 250-255.

Gilson, E., *The Unity of Philosophical Experience*, Charles Scribner's Sons, New York, 1948.

————, "Historical Research and the Future of Scholasticism," *The Modern Schoolman*, vol. 29, No. 1, (November, 1951), pp. 1-10.

Gregory, T. S., "The Philosophy of Fiction," *Dublin Review*, vol. 224, No. 449, 1950, pp. 13-30.

Hardon, J. A., "John Dewey, Prophet of American Naturalism," *Catholic Educational Review*, vol. 50, (September, 1952), pp. 433-445.

Joad, C., *A Critique of Logical Positivism*, University of Chicago Press, Chicago, 1950.

Joergensen, J., *The Development of Logical Empiricism*, International Encyclopedia of United Science, vol. II, No. 9, University of Chicago Press, Chicago, 1951.

Jordan, Z., *The Development of Mathematical Logic and of Logical Positivism in Poland between the Two Wars*, Oxford University Press, New York, 1945.

Kraft, V., *The Vienna Circle*, The Philosophical Library, New York, 1953.

Lewis, C. J., "Logical Positivism and Metaphysics," *The New Scholasticism*, vol. 16, 1942, pp. 242-256.

Maritain, J., *Science and Wisdom*, The Centenary Press, Geoffrey Bles, London, 1944, pp. 3-133.

————, "On Human Knowledge," *Thought*, vol. 24, (June, 1949), pp. 225-243.

————, "On Knowledge Through Connaturality," *The Review of Metaphysics*, vol. 4, (June, 1951), pp. 473-481.

Maurer, A., "Revived Aristotelianism and Thomistic Philosophy," *A History of Philosophical Systems*, ed. V. Ferm, The Philosophical Library, New York, 1950, pp. 197-211.

Moore, E. C., "Positivism and Potentiality," *Journal of Philosophy*, vol. 48, (July, 1951), pp. 472-479.

Morgan, D. N., "Early Modern Empiricism," *A History of Philosophical Systems*, ed. V. Ferm, The Philosophical Library, New York, 1950, pp. 253-265.

Nagel, E., "The Fight for Clarity: Logical Empiricism," *The American Scholar*, vol. 8, No. 1, pp. 45-59.

Noël, L., "The Realism of St. Thomas," *Blackfriars*, vol. 16, 1935, pp. 817-832.

O'Briend-Thomond, A. H., "Positivism and Monism in International Law," *The Franciscan Studies*, vol. 8, 1948, pp. 321-350.

O'Grady, D. C., "Thomism as a Frame of Reference," *The Thomist*, vol. 1, No. 2, 1939, pp. 213-236.

Passmore, J. A., "Descartes, the British Empiricists, and Formal Logic," *The Philosophical Review*, vol. 62, (October, 1953), pp. 545-553.

Pegis, A. C., "The Frontiers of Philosophy and the Limitations of Science," *Proceedings of the American Catholic Philosophical Association*, vol. 11, 1935, pp. 24-37.

Quine, W. V., "Two Dogmas of Empiricism," *The Philosophical Review*, vol. 60, 1951, pp. 20-43.

Randall, Jr., J. H., "The Nature of Naturalism," *Naturalism and the Human Spirit*, ed. Y. H. Krikorian, Columbia University Press, New York, 1946, pp. 354-382.

Ritchie, A. D., "Errors of Logical Positivism," *Philosophy*, vol. 12, 1937, pp. 47-60.

Rousselot, P., *The Intellectualism of St. Thomas*, translated by J. E. O'Mahony, Sheed and Ward, London, 1935.

Santillana, G. de and Zilsel, E., *The Development of Rationalism and Empiricism*, International Encyclopedia of Unified Science, University of Chicago Press, Chicago, vol. II, No. 8, 1953.

Sellars, R. W., "Positivism and Materialism," *Philosophy and Phenomenological Research*, vol. 7, (September, 1946), pp. 12-40.

Smith, J. W., "Progmatism, Realism and Positivism in the United States," *Mind*, vol. 61, (April, 1952), pp. 190-208.

Thayer, H. S., "Two Theories of Truth: the Relation between the Theories of John Dewey and Bertrand Russell," *Journal of Philosophy*, vol. 44, (September, 1947), pp. 516-527.

Thompson, M. H., "J. S. Mill's Theory of Truth," *The Philosophical Review*, vol. 56, 1947, pp. 273-292.

Veatch, H., "Aristotelianism," *A History of Philosophical Systems*, ed. V. Ferm, The Philosophical Library, New York, 1950, pp. 106-117.

Weinberg, J., *An Examination of Logical Positivism*, Harcourt, Brace and Co., New York, 1936.

Wiener, P. P., *Evolution and the Founders of Pragmatism,* Harvard University Press, Cambridge, 1949.

Werkmeister, W. H., "Seven Theses of Logical Positivism Critically Examined," *The Philosophical Review,* vol. 46, 1937, pp. 276-297.

Woodger, J. H., *The Technique of Theory Construction,* International Encyclopedia of Unified Science, vol. II, No. 5, University of Chicago Press, Chicago, 1947.

Ziegelmeyer, E. H., "Comte and Positivism," *The Modern Schoolman,* vol. 20, No. 1, pp. 6-17.

CHAPTER XV
Propaganda

Propaganda and Logic

An introduction to logic would be incomplete without a word to the student about the importance of distinguishing between logic and propaganda. Propaganda is not science, said Hitler, who was a master at the former. Logic, we have come to understand, is the science of thought, the study of reason, an investigation of the acts of the mind by which it apprehends concepts, unites these in the act of judgment, and through judgments reaches certitude or truth. It is the sum total of man's rational processes by which he not only knows but thinks about what he knows. Propaganda, on the other hand (the term is being used here in its modern-day connotation, not in the now obsolete dictionary sense of "imparting information, knowledge, or truth"), is not a system of thought but a system for controlling thought. It might be defined formally as a method utilized for influencing the behavior of others in behalf of particular predetermined ends, or as a systematic attempt to propagate an idea, a doctrine, or a practice for the purpose of controlling the attitudes and consequently the conduct of others. Propaganda, in this sense, might not improperly be described as *subjective* and *ulterior*, and logic as *objective* and *manifest*. In logic the emphasis is on knowing, on certitude, on truth; in propaganda the emphasis is on influence, persuasion, motivation.

Logic and Propaganda

Logic and propaganda, although distinct things in themselves, not infrequently rub shoulders. The propagandist may make use of logic, if only in the sense that he makes use of his audience's ignorance of logical processes. That is to say, he may make use of the illogical. Perhaps few will disagree that propaganda, as we meet it and know it in our own day, is usually illogical. Witness international political propaganda from all sides of the past decade. Witness campaign oratory. Witness advertising and promotion schemes on television, radio, in newspapers and magazines. China is right and America is right; China is wrong and America is wrong. Candidate X will lower taxes and candidate Y will lower taxes; candidate X will spend more for defense and candidate Y will spend more for defense. Luckyfield cigarettes are best and Chestergold cigarettes are best; in fact, more people smoke Luckyfields than Chestergolds smoke people.

Logic and propaganda do sometimes come together, and when the logic is truly logic the impact is not always cushioned. Is propaganda, then, always bad? In the sense that it is not logic, yes. When propaganda becomes logic it is no longer propaganda but *education*. Education *gives* the truth; it does not *use* the truth, in the way that propaganda does. The propagandist seeks to deny men their rational, judicial, critical faculties. The educator recognizes that the truth is its own persuasion.

What is the attitude of the logical man toward propaganda? He is cautious of it. He is on guard against it. He prepares his mind to defend itself against the excesses of distortion and of fallacy. He knows when he encounters them the implements of the special-pleader: a) the propositional fallacies,[19] b) the fallacies of deductive reasoning,[20] c) the weaknesses of the respective techniques of inductive inference.[21] In short, he *uses logic* as a defense against propaganda. When he encounters the pressure of propaganda he takes three measures. First: he looks into the origin of this pressure. He asks, "What is its proximate origin; how did it reach me, of itself, with the aid of someone, by the aim of someone?" He asks, "What is its ultimate origin; who or what has helped it reach me, or made it reach me?" Second: he looks into the purpose of the pressure. He asks "What is the end, the view, the goal offered or suggested? Is it individual, is it social? Is it for the good of some *one* or of all, in the sense that truth is for the good of all? Third: having answered these questions for himself, he applies as a gauge all that he has learned about orderly, clear, right, correct, and true thinking. That is to say, in fine, he applies the principles of logic.

"Propaganditis," Its Care and Cure

A last word needs to be said about keeping a sense of proportion. A right attitude toward propaganda is one thing; a phobia about it is another. Unhappy is the citizen who spends his days figuring out how the radio, the press, the cinema, television, the world, and everybody in it is conspiring to put something over on him. Only less happy are those who have to live with him. The world is full of propagandists, of distorters, of special-pleaders, but it is also full of apostles of the truth. Full of those who want to find truth and to give truth. Truth, like goodness, is overflowing; it wants to spread itself. And when a logician grabs you by the coat lapel, think twice before you suppose it's to steal the flower in your button-hole. The logical mind does not sit quiet. It is not passive or timid, but assertive and bold, its goal being knowledge, certitude, truth. Nevertheless, though it is all these things, it is at the same time cognizant that there are other minds around it, that it is the nature of all minds to seek knowledge, to try to know, and that (as pointed out near the very outset of this book) of none, more than of the logical mind, might we expect a wholesome tolerance of the free working of other minds.

SUPPLEMENTARY READINGS FOR CHAPTER XV

Catlin, G. E. G., "Propaganda as a Function of Democratic Government," *Propaganda and Dictatorship*, ed. H. L. Childs, Princeton University Press, Princeton, 1936, pp. 125-145.

Childs, H. L., "The Place of Propaganda in Modern Life," *The Annals of the American Academy of Political and Social Science*, vol. 179, (May, 1935), pp. 187-239.

Doob, L. W., "The Nature of Propaganda," *Propaganda*, Henry Holt and Co., New York, 1935, pp. 71-151.

————, "The Sweep of Propaganda," *Propaganda*, Henry Holt and Co., New York, 1935, pp. 155-330.

————, *Public Opinion and Propaganda*, Henry Holt, New York, 1948.

Fried, E., "Techniques of Persuasion," *Propaganda by Short Wave*, ed. H. L. Childs and J. B. Whitton, Princeton University Press, Princeton, 1943, pp. 263-301.

Henderson, E. H., "Toward a Definition of Propaganda," *Journal of Psychology*, vol. 18, 1943, pp. 71-87.

Jacob, P. C., "Atrocity Propaganda," *Propaganda by Short Wave*, ed. H. L. Childs and J. B. Whitton, Princeton University Press, Princeton, 1943, pp. 211-259.

Lasswell, H. D., Casey, R. D., Smith, B. L., *Propaganda and Promotional Activities: An Annotated Bibliography*, University of Minnesota Press, Minneapolis, 1935.

Lavine, H., and Wachsler, J., *War Propaganda and the United States*, Yale University Press, New Haven, 1940.

Lerner, M., *Ideas Are Weapons, the History and Uses of Ideas*, The Viking Press, New York, 1939.

Lumley, F. E., *The Propaganda Menace*, Appleton-Century-Crofts, New York, 1933.

Maxwell, B. M., "Political Propaganda in Soviet Russia," *Propaganda and Dictatorship*, ed. H. L. Childs, Princeton University Press, Princeton, 1936, pp. 61-79.

Meaney, J. W., "Propaganda as Physical Coercion," *Review of Politics*, University of Notre Dame, Notre Dame, Indiana, vol. 13, (January, 1951), pp. 64-87.

Riegel, O. W., *Mobilizing for Chaos*, Yale University Press, New Haven, 1934.

FOOTNOTES TO PART FOUR

1. *The Dictionary of Philosophy*, ed. D. D. Runes, The Philosophical Library, New York, 1942, pp. 196-7.
2. J. S. Mill, *System of Logic*, Longmans, Green, and Co., 1895, pp. 253-266.
3. *Ibid.*, p. 365.
4. F. C. Dillhoff, *How Is Scholastic Logic Facing Modern Logic?* Ph.D. dissertation, University of Pittsburgh, 1952.
5. C. J. Ducasse, *Philosophy in American Education*, Harper & Brothers, New York, 1945, pp. 224-227.
6. P. Boehner, O.F.M., *Medieval Logic*, University of Chicago Press, Chicago, 1952, pp. 95-96.
7. Aristotle, *De Sophisticis Elenchis*, 165a 5-10.
8. *Encyclopaedia Britannica*, 14th ed., vol. 14, 1948, p. 330.
9. A. M. Frye, A. W. Levi, *Rational Belief*, Harcourt, Brace and Co., New York, 1941, pp. 7-18.
10. R. Carnap, *Introduction to Semantics*, Harvard University Press, Cambridge, 1942, p. 9.
11. See above, ch. III, p. 30.
12. See above, ch. III, p. 32.
13. J. H. Randall, Jr., "The Nature of Naturalism," *Naturalism and the Human Spirit*, ed. Y H. Krikorian, Columbia University Press, New York, 1944, p. 369.
14. *Ibid.*, p. 374.
15. Randall, *op. cit.*, p. 381.
16. R. Carnap, "Testability and Meaning," *Readings in the Philosophy of Science*, ed. H. Feigl and M. Brodbeck, Appleton-Century-Crofts, Inc., New York, 1953, pp. 84-86.
17. D. C. O'Grady, "Thomism as a Frame of Reference," *The Thomist*, vol. 1, 1939, p. 228.
18. *Ibid.*, pp. 234-5.
19. See above, ch. VIII, p. 71.
20. See above, ch. XI, p. 96f.
21. See above, ch. XII, p. 108f, 112, 113.

INDEX

A

ABRAHAM, L., 99
Abstraction, 19, 20, 139
Accidental, see contingent
ADLER, M., 66
AIKINS., H. A., 8
ALDRICH, V. C., 34, 66
Algebra of logic, xiv, 122
ALLERS, R., 42
Analogy, 112-114
ANDERSON, F. H., 129, 140
Antecedent, 82, 85, 89
A posteriori, 109, 139
Apprehension, simple, 16-21
A priori, 109, 139
A-proposition, 59, 89
ARDLEY, G., 129
Argumentation, 81, 84
ARISTOTLE, xv, 2, 29, 41, 51, 66, 73, 99, 101, 102, 116, 122, 123, 124, 149
ASCHENBRENNER, K., 34
ASHER, M., 116
ASHLEY, B. M., 118, 131
Assent, 46
Assortment and division, 46
AUGUSTINE, 49
AVEY, A. E., 8, 129
AYER, A. J., 34, 140

B

BACON, F., 110, 116
Baconian tables, 110
BAIER, K., 42
BAHM, A. J., 99
BAKAN, M. B., 72
BALLARD, E. S., 34
BASSON, A. H., 34
BARNES, W. H. F., 140
BAYLIS, C. A., 66
BEARDSLEY, E. L., 66
BEARDSLEY, M. C. 8
Being, 15, 16
    defined, 22

BENJAMIN, A. C., 116, 140
BENNETT, O., 99
BENTLEY, A. F., 129, 140
BERENDA, C. W., 140
BERGMANN, G., 130, 140
BISBEE, E., 66
BITTLE, C. N., 42
BLACK, M., 34, 66, 99
BLOOMFIELD, L., 116
BOCHENSKI, I. M., 99, 101, 102, 125, 130
BOEHNER, P., 8, 34, 51, 130, 149
BOGOSLOVSKY, B. B., 9
BOOLE, G., 8, 130
BOURKE, V. J., 21
BRADY, I., 130
BRIDGMAN, P. W., 116
BRITTON, K., 35
BROAD, C. D., 21
BRODBECK, M., 140
BROWN, H. C., 35
BROWN, R., 66
BUCHDAHL, G., 116
BUCHLER, J., 140
BURKS, A. W., 26, 116
BURTT, E. A., 9

C

Canons, Mill's, 110-112
CARMICHAEL, P. A., 116
CARNAP, R., 117, 130, 149
CASEY, R. D., 148
Categorical proposition, 57
Categories, 48
CATLIN, G. E. G., 148
Cause, 110, 114
Cause and effect, 107, 110, 114
CERF, W., 140
CHASE, S., 35
CHATALIAN, G., 117
CHILDS, H. L., 148
CHESTERTON, G. K., 129
CHISHOLM, R. M., 140
CHURCH, A., 130

151

CHURCHMAN, C. W., 99, 117, 130
CHWISTEK, L., 117
CLARK, J. T., 67, 117, 130
COFFEY, B., 117
COHEN, M. R., 117
COLLINS, J., 67
Completeness, 49, 71
Components, see notes
  of being, 22-23
  of judgment, 47
  of mental argumentation, 81- 82
  of mental statement, 53
  of proposition, 55
  of syllogism, 84-85
Comprehension, 22, 23, 24
COMTE, A., 138
Concept, 5, 19, 42
  defined, 22
  divided, 25-26
Conclusion, 85
Condition, 114
CONNOLLY, F. G., 21, 140
Consequence, 82, 101
Consequent, 82, 85, 89
Constant, 31, 55, 81
  defined, 31
  divided, 31
Context, xiv, 32
Contingency, contingent or accidental, 23, 58, 64
Contradiction, contradictory, 60, 63, 64, 65, 70
Contrapositional, 62
Contrariety, contrary, 61, 63, 64, 65
Conversion, 62, 70, 90
  defined, 62
  divided, 62
COOLEY, J. C., 130
COPILOWISH, I. M., 41, 67
COPLESTON, F. C., 67, 130, 140
Copula, 31, 47, 55
CORCORAN, J. D., 118, 131
COUTURAT, L., 130
CREED, I. P., 99
CREEDY, F., 9
CUNNINGHAM, G. W., 130

D

DALTON, J., 115
DAWSON, C., 141

Deduction, 79, 137
Definition, 37-39
  defined, 37
  divided, 38
De MORGAN, A., 130
DEWEY, J., 35, 41, 51, 67, 141
Dilemma, 95
DILLHOFF, F. C., xv, xviii, 149
Division, 39-41
  defined, 40
  divided, 40
DOOB, L. W., 148
DOTTERER, R. H., 117
DOYLE, J. J., 67
DUBS, H. H., 41, 99, 117
DUCASSE, C. J., xiv, 67, 117, 149
DUNNE, P., 26
DÜRR, K., 130

E

EATON, R. M., 130
EDWARDS, P., 67, 99
Effect, 107, 110, 114
Emotional, meaning, context, xiv, 34
Empiricism, see positivism
ENRIQUES, R., 131
Enthymeme, 92, 93
E-proposition, 59, 89
Equivalence, 66, 70
ESLICK, L. J., 67
Essence, 18, 47
Essential, see necessary
EVANS, I., 131
Experimentation, 109-112
Extension, 24

F

Fallacy, 71, 96, 146
  propositional, 71
  syllogistic, 96
Falsity, 16, 49
FARBER, M., 131, 141
FEIBLEMAN, J. K., 131, 141
FEIGL, H., 117, 118, 141
FERM, V., 141
Figure, 87, 91
FLEW, A. G. N., 35
Form, matter, 25, 82, 124
FOSTER, M. H., 35
FRANK, P., 141

INDEX

FRANKEL, C., 141
FREGE, G., 131
FRIED, E., 148
FRYE, A. M., 149

G

GALLAGHER, D., 141
GALLIE, W. B., 141
GARNETT, A. C., 141
GEACH, P. T., 51, 131
GENTRY, G., 35
GILSON, E., 142
GOMPREZ, H., 35
GOODMAN, N., 67
GRAY, L. H., 131
GREENWOOD, T., 67, 99, 118, 131
GREGORY, T. S., 142
GUTHRIE, E. R., 9

H

HAMILTON, W., 42
HARDON, J. A., 142
HARROD, H. R. F., 118
HART, C. A., xviii
HEMPEL, C. G., 118
HENDERSON, E. H., 148
HENLE, P., 99
HERBERG, W., 131
HESS, M. W., 131
HIZ, H., 72
HOENEN, P., 51, 67
HOFSTADTER, A., 118, 131
HUNTINGTON, E. V., 118
Hypothesis, 108, 114, 115

I

Idea, see concept
Identity, principle of, 4
  triple, 85
I-proposition, 59, 89
Impossibility, impossible, 58, 59
Impossible, reduction by, 90, 91
Indemonstrable, first, 4, 5, 21
  second, 19, 20
Induction, 97, 105, 137
Inference, immediate, 69, 70, 71, 77, 89
  mediate, 69, 108
Insoluble, 121, 128
Integration, 59, 60, 89
ISENBERG, A., 35

J

JACOB, P. C., 148
JACOBY, P., 67
JOAD, C., 142
JOERGENSEN, J., 142
JOHN of ST. THOMAS, 42
JOHNSON, A. B., 35
JOHNSTONE, H. W., 99
JORDAN, Z., 142
JOSEPH, H. B., 131
Judgment, 45, 46, 79, 80, 139

K

KANE, W. H., 118, 131
KAPLAN, A., 67
KATTSOFF, L. O., 131
KAPP, E., 51, 99, 118
KAUFMANN, F., 51, 118
KECSKEMETI, P., 35
KELLY, A. D., 132
KEYNES, J. N., 8, 118
KIMPEL, B. F., 9
KING, H. R., 132
KLUBERTANZ, G. P., 99
KNEALE, W., 118, 132
KNIGHT, F. H., 118
Knowing, knowledge, 5, 16, 18, 21, 107, 108, 139, 145
  modes of, 37
KOCOUREK, R. A., 118, 132
KORZYBSKI, A., 132
KRAFT, V., 142

L

LACHANCE, L., 35
LAFLEUR, L. J., 72
LANGFORD, C. H., 132
Language, 31, 125, 126, 127
LARGUIER, E. H., 132
LASSWELL, H. D., 148
LAVINE, H., 148
Law, 114
  of all and none, 86, 98
  of argumentation, 83
  of being, 4
  of contradiction, 4, 5
  of identity, 4, 5
  of logical tolerance, 19, 21, 148
  of separating third, 85
  of the excluded middle, 4, 5
  of thought, 4, 106
  of triple identity, 85

LEBLANC, H., 41, 132
LEBLOND, J., 132
LEE, H. N., 35
LERNER, M., 148
LEVI, A. W., 149
LEWIS, C. J., 132, 142
LOEWENBERG, J., 26
Logic, 1-8, 127, 145
  and propaganda, 145
  formal, 2
  material, 2
  mathematical, xiv, xv, 2, 122
  philosophical, 2
  old and new, 121-129
  symbolic, xiv, 122, 123
  traditional, xiii, xiv, xv, 122, 139
Logical empiricism, positivism, 107, 136, 138
Logical truth, see truth
Logistics, 122
LUKASIEWICZ, J., 100, 102
LUMLEY, F. E., 148

M
MABBOTT, J. D., 100
MacPARTLAND, J., 21
MARITAIN, J., 8, 73, 118, 142
MARKENKEE, P., 68
MATES, B., 132
Mathematical logic, xiv, xv, 2, 122
Mathematization, 106
Matter, form, 25, 82, 124
MAURER, A., 142
MAXWELL, B. M., 148
Mc CALL, R. J., 73
Mc GILL, V. J., 9, 35
Mc WILLIAMS, J. A., 118
MEANEY, J. W., 149
Meaning, 18, 34, 47
MENGER, K., 100, 119, 132
Mental, mental being, see concept
  argumentation, 81
  statement, 53
  word, 22
MESTHENE, E. G., 132
Method, 5, 145
  scientific, 99, 115, 123
MEYER, J., 35
Middle term, 85, 86, 87
  defined, 85
MILL, J. S., xiii, 110, 119, 149

MILLER, J. W., 132
MINOGUE, G. P., 72
Modal,
  proposition, 57
  syllogism, 92
MONTAGUE, W. P., 9, 132
Mood, mode, 87, 88, 90, 91
MOODY, E. A., 35, 100, 132
MOORE, E. C., 142
MOORE, T. V., 21
MOORE, W., 35
MORGAN, D. N., 142
MULLALLY, J. P., 36
MULLER-THYM, B., 51
MURRAY, J., 26

N
NAGEL, E., 9, 51, 117, 133, 142
Nature, see essence
Naturalism, 107, 136, 137
Necessity, necessary or essential, 23, 58, 63
NEGLEY, G. R., 9
NEWMAN, J. H., 68, 72
NICOD, J., 119
NOEL, L., 143
NOGAR, R. J., 118, 131
Notes, 22, 23, 24, 42

O
Observation, 108, 109
O'BRIEN-THOMOND, A. H., 143
Obversion, 66, 70
Occasion, 114
OCKHAM, W., of, 122
O'CONNOR, D. J., 36
OESTERLE, J. A., 36, 133
OGDEN, C. K., 36, 41
O'GRADY, D. C., 133, 143, 149
OLIVER, W. D., 68
O'MARA, J., 21
O'NEIL, J. M., 133
Ontology, ontological, xvii, 3
Operations and products of the mind, xvii, 7
Opposition of propositions, 60
O-proposition, 59, 89
O'TOOLE, G. B., 51

P
Paradox, 121, 128
PARRY, W. T., 100

INDEX

PASSMORE, J. A., 143
PEGIS, A. C., 143
PEIFER, J. F., 26
PEPPER, S. C., 41
PERKINS, M., 51
Phantasm, 19
PHILIPOV, A., 133
Philosophy, 2
PLATO, 8
PLOCKMANN, G. K., 100
Polysyllogism, 95
POPKIN, R., 41, 100
POPOV, P. S., 9
Possibility, possible, 57, 59
Positivism, logical, 107, 136, 138
POST, E. L., 133
Predicaments, 48
Predicate, 49
Predication, 46
Premise, 85, 89
Principle, 3, 114
   first, 3
   of all and none, 86, 98
   of argumentation, 83
   of being, 4
   of contradiction, 4, 5
   of identity, 4, 5
   of logical tolerance, 19, 21, 148
   of separating third, 85
   of the excluded middle, 4, 5
   of thought, 4, 106
   of triple identity, 85
PRIOR, A. N., 133
Propaganda, 145
Propaganditis, 148
Proper, 18
Properties, 23
   of concepts, 22
   of judgments, 49
   of propositions, 60
   of terms, 32
Proposition, 55-66, 89
   defined, 55
   divided, 57
   nature of true affirmative, 56
Psychology, psychological, xvii, 3

Q

Quality of proposition, 57
Quantity of proposition, 58
Quiddity, see essence
QUINE, W. V., 26, 36, 68, 100, 125, 133, 143

R

RANDALL, J. H., 143, 149
READE, W. H. V., 100
Reasoning, 77, 79
   deductive, 79
   inductive, 79
   by analogy, 112
Reduction, 90
REICHENBACH, H., 100, 119
REID, J. R., 41, 42
REISER, O., 9
Relations of propositions, 60
RIEGEL, O. W., 149
RICHARDS, I. A., 36, 41, 72
RITCHIE, A. D., 119, 133, 143
RITTER, W. E., 133
ROBINSON, R., 42
ROONEY, M., 133
ROSENBLOOM, P., 133
ROSS, A., 68
ROSS, W. D., 100
ROUGIER, L., 134
ROUSSELOT, P., 143
Rules of categorical syllogism, 86, 87
RUSSELL, B., 68, 125, 135
RYAN, J. K., 42

S

SABINE, G. H., 134
SANTILLANA, G. de, 143
SCHORSCH, A., 119
Scientific,
   empiricism, see positivism
   method, 99, 115, 123
SCOTUS, D., 122
SEARLES, H. L., 134
SELLARS, R. W., 52, 143
Semantics, 121, 125
Semiotic, 138
SESMAT, A., 42
SHELDON, W. H., 68
SHUR, E., 100
SIDWICK, A., 72
Sign, 28
   defined, 29
   divided, 29, 30
Signification, 29, 30, 32, 126, 129

SIMON, Y. R., 100
SINGER, M. G., 134
SISSON, E. O., 26, 52
SMITH, B. L., 148
SMITH, G., 27, 52
SMITH, H. B., 68, 72
SMITH, J. W., 143
SMITH, M., 119
SMITH, V. E., 119, 134
SOLMSEN, F., 100
Sorites, 93
SPAULDING, E. G., 68
SPILSBURY, R. J., 119
SPRAGUE, R. K., 21
STAKELUM, J. W., 100
STEBBING, L. S., 72
STEVENSON, C. C., 36
STEVENSON, C. L., 42
STRAWSON, P. F., 119, 134
Subalternation, 61, 62, 63, 64, 65
Sub-contrariety, sub-contrary, 61, 63, 64, 65
Subject, 47, 53, 56
Substance, 47
SULLIVAN, H., 119
Supposition, 33, 34, 129
SUTFIN, E., 134
Syllogism, 84-99
   defined, 84
   divided, 84
Symbolization, 123, 124

T

TALIAFERRO, R. C., 134
TALLON, H. J., 68
TARSKI, A., 52
Technique, experimental, 109-112
Term, 30-34
   defined, 30
   divided, 31
THAYER, H. S., 52, 143
Theory, 115
Thinking, 1, 4, 5, 6, 7, 18, 54, 78
THOMAS AQUINAS, xv, xviii, 8, 42, 49, 52, 102, 119, 122
THOMAS, I., 134
THOMPSON, M. H., 52, 68, 134, 143
Tolerance, logical, 21, 148
TOMS, E., 9
TOOHEY, J. J., 52, 100

TOULMIN, S. E., 42
Truth, xvii, 5, 16, 49, 50, 79, 106, 147
TYRRELL, F. M., 52

U

Unity, 49
USHENKO, A. P., 119, 134

V

VAN DER VELT, J., 21
Variable, 31, 55, 81
   defined, 31
   divided, 55
   propositional, 81, 101
VEATCH, H. B., 27, 36, 68, 100, 101, 119, 134, 135, 143
VENN, J., 135
VON WRIGHT, G. H., 119

W

WACHSLER, J., 148
WALCOTT, G. D., 119
WALKER, E. R., 119
WALPOLE, H. R., 135
WALSH, F. A., 21, 72, 135
WALTON, W. M., 68
WANG, H., 119
WATLING, J., 66
WEAVER, W., 119
WEINBERG, J. R., 68, 143
WEINER, P. P., 36, 144
WELLMUTH, J., 72, 135
WERKMEISTER, W. H., 144
WESTAWAY, F. W., 119
WHITEHEAD, A. N., 135
WHITTAKER, J. F., 135
WICK, W. A., 135
WIGHTMAN, W. P .D., 119
WILD, J., 21
WILL, F. L., 101
WILSON, J. C., 101, 119
WITTGENSTEIN, L., 135
WOLF, A., 119
WOODGER, J. H., 144
WOODWORTH, R. S., 21
WORDSWORTH, xvii

Y

YOUNG, T., 134

Z

ZIEGELMEYER, E. H., 144
ZILSEL, E., 143